The
Homework
Solution

Linda Sonna, PH.D.

Williamson Publishing Company   Charlotte, Vermont

Dr. Linda Agler Sonna is a clinical psychologist in Dallas, Texas, where she has also taught and counseled in the public schools. She has written, counseled and spoken extensively to both professional and general audiences on the homework solution program.

Library of Congress
Cataloging-in-Publication Data

Sonna, Linda Agler, 1950-
    The homework solution / Linda Agler Sonna.
            p.   cm.
    Includes bibliographical references (p.).
    ISBN 0-913589-52-7: $9.95
    1. Homework 2. Study, Method of. 3. Education—Parent participation. I. Title.
LB1048.S67 1990
649'.68—dc20 90-34235

Cover design: Trezzo-Braren Studio
Typography: LaserImage
Printer: Capital City Press

Williamson Publishing Co.
P.O. Box 185
Charlotte, Vermont 05445
1-800-234-8791

Manufactured in the United States of America

10 9 8 7

Notice: The information contained in this book is true, complete, and accurate to the best of our knowledge. All recommendations and suggestions are made without any guarantees on the part of the author or Williamson Publishing. The author and publisher disclaim all liability incurred in connection with the use of this information.

Contents

To William Lee Sonna

My brother Bill didn't do homework in elementary school despite my parents' efforts to encourage, cajole, persuade, bribe, and punish. He didn't succeed in junior high school despite their help. At age 15, Bill joined the ranks of the high school drop-outs.

Less typically, Bill later entered the University of Illinois and completed his master's degree in civil engineering. He plans to place his children on this homework program as soon as they are old enough to attend nursery school!

A wise mother considers her children's successes to be hers, and their failures their own.

Lois "Mom" Sonna

Preface

If you are like most parents, one of your scarcest commodities is time. Attending to your youngster's homework takes up a good deal of your time during the week.

You spend time asking about homework: "Do you have any assignments tonight?" "Is there a test tomorrow?" "How's your term paper coming along?"

You spend time reminding about homework: "Bring your math home tonight so we can work on it." " Time to study!" "Don't forget you have a test on Friday."

You spend time helping: "I marked the problems you need to redo. The directions say you must refer to the chart on page 12." "The capital of Greece is Athens."

You spend time lecturing and setting limits: "No T.V. until you finish your homework." "If you don't study, you'll fail!" "Time to put your books away and get some rest."

You also spend time doubting yourself: "Am I expecting too much or too little?" "Are the teachers demanding too much or too little?" "Is my child trying too hard or not hard enough?"

And you spend time worrying: "Will he pass the year if he doesn't buckle down?" "Would her grades improve if she studied harder?" "Is he putting too much pressure on himself?"

You even spend time worrying about your worries: "Am I overly concerned about these problems?" "Am I worrying needlessly?"

Keeping tabs on a child who tries to wiggle out of doing homework can be frustrating and exhausting. When poor study habits hinder academic progress, a child's future may be on the line. Overachievers may place so much pressure to succeed on themselves that they endanger their physical and emotional health. When the homework problems are one of many difficulties a child is having, parents may feel overwhelmed and confused as to how to intervene.

To respond to these dilemmas, I have developed a homework program with the following goals:

★ To teach children to accept responsibility for homework and studying

★ To reduce parent-child conflicts over homework

★ To help children develop the attitudes and behaviors that enable them to do homework and study to the best of their abilities

★ To motivate children to study and do homework to the best of their abilities.

Almost every child can be taught to do homework responsibly. In the following chapters, parents, teachers and counselors are shown how to set the stage to prevent homework problems before they begin, and how to help students overcome destructive study habits that have developed over a period of many years.

This program may be used with children entering first grade to seniors completing their last semester of high school. The academically gifted, the average child, and those with learning problems can all be taught the skills and helped to develop the attitudes necessary to accept responsibility, so they can do their homework.

Parents can implement this program regardless of their own academic background, knowledge of particular school subjects, or economic level. Although homework is a complex subject and every student has different educational and emotional needs and learning abilities, this program is designed so that the structure and attention children receive make it a positive experience for them.

I know of no magic that can turn a below-average child into an A student or help a student suddenly overcome years of accumulated academic deficiencies. On my homework program, however, students usually begin accepting responsibility and actually doing their homework in about two weeks. To allow enough time for studying to become a part of the student's daily routine, parents must make a major investment of time and energy for about a month. This will be a difficult sacrifice for parents who are single, have other commitments in the evenings, or have younger children at home. Since siblings have to forego some of their parent's time and attention during this period, they will be making a sacrifice as well. This united effort to resolve homework problems results in a major saving of time and energy in the long run, brings families closer together, and can make home a happier place, once homework struggles are eliminated.

This study program cannot help children who are so out of control that parents would have to use physical force to keep them at a study table. Such youngsters require psychotherapy to help them develop better self-control. Then, they, too, can benefit from these techniques.

Many parents who were sure they would have to use physical restraints or corporal punishment to gain their children's cooperation have been surprised to discover how amenable their youngsters are to following this program. Therefore, I recommend parents think carefully before assuming "it won't work." Most children are as pleased to have help overcoming their homework problems as are their parents. It is a serious error to assume that non-studiers like to be that way!

As presented, the program is highly structured and some of the recommended measures may seem extreme. I have presented it in this way for students who have particularly serious and long-standing homework problems. Most parents will not need to follow all of the procedures or employ all of the techniques discussed. For instance, many parents find that simply sitting down with their children while they study is enough to bring about significant improvements in children's attention to their studies. Parents who alter the way they communicate with their youngsters about homework often note tremendous changes in attitude, especially among adolescents.

I developed this solution to the homework problem when counseling families in which one or more children were having homework problems. The excellent results I have observed are due to the steadfast commitment of parents, the readiness of teachers to respond to students' needs, and the willingness of children to seize the opportunity to learn.

My work brought me into on-going contact with schools, and I have been continually impressed by the exceptional dedication of teachers to furthering their students' best interests. I learned that when teachers appear unresponsive or uncaring, it is most often because they are over-whelmed by the many pressures to which they are subjected. Still, most teachers are willing to extend themselves to meet the needs of individual students. My contacts with students have taught me that it is a rare child who doesn't want to please teachers and parents, and to succeed. Those that seem set on a path of failure are either having other problems or simply don't know how to correct their situation. My work with parents has shown me that they truly value education and want their children to do well in school. Despite crowded schedules and overwhelming responsibilities, most parents put a lot of time and energy into their youngster's studies.

It is when these three groups do not remain in close communication that a cycle of blame often develops which serves to worsen the very problems everyone is trying to solve. My greatest hope is that teachers, parents, and children can remember that only by working together can they accomplish the most important goal: to help every student become the best he or she can be.

Special thanks to the many who supported my efforts to complete this manuscript by opening up their homes to me: Loyce and Lauren Easterly, Joy Urban, Lois and Abe Mark, Mark-Brian Sonna, Larry Groseclose, and

Alex Mittelman. And I wish to thank Jan Winebrenner, Jay Gaines, John Millerman, Diane Gilliard, William Sonna, Stephen Scherrffius, Leroy Howe, Fred Dea Entriken, Mark Farley and Greg Popek for their continuing encouragement. Most of all, thanks to the many students who helped me see the world through their eyes.

Chapter 1

A Simple, Direct Solution

Do you know a child who develops mysterious wrist cramps when required to write an essay? Who forgets his books at school when he's supposed to study for a test? Who puts as much energy into struggling over homework as doing it? If so, you may be involved with a student who is suffering from a scourge running rampant among elementary, middle school, and high school pupils. I have dubbed it "homework phobia."

This ailment commonly consists of an intense, continuing aversion to doing school work at home. It usually strikes children between second and sixth grades, but has been known to begin as early as first grade and last through high school. (Those who don't overcome it rarely make it to college.)

Another pattern is displayed by perfectionists who are overly obsessive about their studies. These "homework fanatics" have a hard time knowing when to quit. They suffer insomnia, ulcers, and headaches at a young age. Many show signs of burnout by high school.

Homework phobia results in poor school grades, continuing struggles between parents, teachers, and students, and premature withdrawal from high school. The only positive effect is that the parents of these children become experts on such diverse subjects as the history of eels, factoring of algebraic equations, and sentence diagramming.

The criteria for determining whether a child is afflicted with a homework phobia is a bit tricky since the child may be quite relaxed, happy, and carefree. Children with homework problems run the gamut from academically gifted, to average, to below average. They may or may not have learning disabilities or other problems. Often they are brighter than their school grades would indicate. In fact, children who have homework problems are hard to distinguish from their non-afflicted peers.

The parents of these homework phobic children are the ones likely to be experiencing acute distress. In fact, the easiest way to diagnose homework phobia in a child is to examine the parents. If one or both parents are prone to utter any of the following sentences about once a week during the school year, one or more of their children is probably having homework problems:

★ "No, Johnny! Not after the next T.V. program. Start your homework now."

★ "Really, Johnny. You don't have any homework again tonight?"

★ "What do you mean you forgot your assignments and books at school?"

★ "I'm not doing your work for you! You aren't even trying!"

★ "How will you ever make it through college when I'm not there to hold your hand?"

★ "I don't care what the teacher says! 3 + 3 = 6, not 5!"

★ "You call this homework 'done'? It's a mess and all the answers are wrong!"

★ "But it's after 10:00 p.m.! All the stores are closed! How long have you known you needed a spiral binder by first period tomorrow?"

★ "If you didn't understand the assignment, why didn't you ask the teacher to explain it?"

★ "If your teacher really doesn't care whether or not students do the work, why does he assign it?"

Meanwhile, parents of homework fanatics are struggling with a different set of problems. They are likely to make statements like these:

★ "The world won't come to an end, if you make a mistake or don't do all the extra credit."

★ "What do you mean you're too ill to go to school again today!"

★ "All this worrying is going to make you old before your time."

★ "Listening to you worry is making me old before my time!"

★ "That's enough studying! Call me 'mean' if you must, but I insist you go out and have fun whether you like it or not!"

How This Approach Was Developed

My interest in children's homework problems dates back to 1960 when I was 10 years old. As a conscientious rule follower, I wouldn't have missed doing a homework assignment or studying for a test for all the Barbie dolls in the world. My 8-year-old brother, Bill, on the other hand, was steadfastly indifferent to homework. Bill did homework when and if he felt like it — which was almost never.

I spent my childhood watching my parents spend a large part of every evening "helping" Bill with his homework. The "help" began during dinner when father asked if he had any homework due the next day. Since father never queried me, I supposed the question was really meant as a reminder. Shortly after dinner mother dropped a few gentle hints that Bill should start working on his homework before it got to be too late. Of course, Bill always considered it much too early, but promised to begin "in a few minutes." Several T.V. shows later, mother's reminders became angry commands to "go do it now." When her pleas failed, father stepped in with a more forceful approach. He delivered his customary lecture about the life of poverty and crime which is the fate of all non-studiers, then issued various threats. Dad always promised to carry out the threats the very next time Bill "forgot" to bring his assignment list, books, or study sheets home.

There were many late night dashes to the corner grocery to buy still another set of colored pencils for Bill's geography homework, attempts to get into his school at night to extricate forgotten social studies books from his locker, and hurried trips to the library to check out books for the English report he had failed to mention until the night before the assignment was due.

At the breakfast table my parents conducted daily drills to teach Bill his vocabulary words, state capitals, and math facts. The goal was to try to keep him from failing the next quiz, test, exam, or year in school. When my parents' preoccupation with their own marital difficulties took precedence over Bill's homework problems during ninth grade, he promptly failed all his courses and dropped out.

I must admit I was envious of Bill's ability to capture and hold my parents' attention for several hours each evening and through breakfast most mornings. I also envied the ability of many of my classmates to attract so much attention from the teachers at school using similar techniques of passive resistance. I envied them, but felt resentful over the unfairness of it all. It seemed that the way to get attention from the adults in my world was to break the rules and be a "bad" student. Lacking the courage to seek attention in this way, I vowed to become a teacher when I grew up and devote all my attention to the quiet, studious types like myself who followed the rules, did their homework, and tried to please.

At age 10, I couldn't understand why the solution to Bill's homework problems (that seemed so obvious to me) continued to elude my parents. I wondered why my parents spent so much time worrying about Bill's homework, when I was sure all they needed to do was turn off the T.V. for an hour, make him sit at the kitchen table with nothing but his books for company, and repeat the same scenario every night until Bill realized he couldn't avoid it. I was sure this procedure would motivate him to study, if only to relieve the boredom.

One day I suggested this procedure to my parents, but they just shook their heads. "If only it were as simple as that," mother sighed. "You're just too young to understand how complicated these things are."

What I didn't realize at the time, however, was that my overzealous approach to homework was a problem, too. I was overly bent on being the perfect student. I became upset if I didn't understand how to do an assignment, and sometimes cried if I couldn't figure it out. I had migraine headaches after completing major projects. When my parents held firm about lights out at bedtime, I studied on the sly with a flashlight. No matter how much I did, it never seemed to me to be enough. My parents kept telling me to relax and take it easy, but I couldn't comprehend their meaning. To my way of thinking, I simply wanted to do well in school. Back then, I didn't realize there was such a thing as doing well in life. It wasn't until I finished my education that I realized I had become an adult without ever having been a child.

When I began teaching high school, I soon discovered that many of my students were as resistant to studying and doing homework as my brother Bill had been. Many students failed my Spanish and French classes simply because they didn't do or didn't turn in their homework assignments. Other students received low report card grades because they neglected to do the long-range projects I assigned each semester. And many who were barely passing due to their lackadaisical attitude toward school guaranteed a failing grade by refusing to review for the final exam.

So there I was doing exactly what I had promised myself I'd never do: nagging, lecturing, warning, and meting out various punishments to non-studiers while virtually ignoring my many compliant, motivated students. I was spending so much time reprimanding the ne'er-do-wells about their need to pay attention in class, to study, and to do homework that I had little time left to reward those who participated, completed their assignments, and studied regularly. I considered doing what most of the other teachers did: Send notes home to the parents explaining the assignments and asking them to make sure the work was completed. I realized, however, that many parents would not know enough Spanish or French to be able to monitor their children's work or help them prepare for tests.

I remembered the solution that had seemed so obvious to me when my parents were caught up in endless struggles with my brother and decided to give it a try. I announced to all my classes that I was instituting three new rules:

1. Students who didn't hand in their homework when it was due would be required to stay after school to finish it.

2. Students who received a failing grade on a homework assignment would be required to stay after school to correct missed items and receive additional tutoring.

3. Students who failed a quiz or test would be required to stay after school to retake it until they passed.

I was alarmed by the reaction of the students when I announced these new rules. No one seemed to care! I was threatening to keep them after school, which is a fate worse than death to most high school students, and no one groaned, protested, or even furled a forehead demonstrating concern! I could tell my rules were falling on deaf ears. That meant I would have to stay after school myself until my many non-studiers realized I was serious. I wasn't thrilled at the prospect of having to do this. When the final school bell rang, I was as ready to head for home as anyone else. I quickly realized that my marvelous solution was going to result in as much work for me as for them...that I would have to pay the price for their recalcitrant behavior. After much moaning and groaning about errant teenagers, I decided it was a price I was willing to pay.

To my delight, it took only two weeks of staying after school before every student in every class (over 100 students in total) was doing homework and passing quizzes and tests on the first try! *As soon as everyone realized I really would enforce the rules and make them stay after school every day for the entire school year, everyone complied!* (I must admit I'm not sure I could have brought myself to actually stay after school for the rest of my life, but luckily I never had to put myself to the test.)

I experienced only three problems with my new policy. My biggest battle was with the football coach who tried to pressure me into exempting his athletes for football practice. Although I feared for my job when one student's parents called the principal and he came down to discuss the matter with me, I remained obstinate and employed. Within a few weeks, the student raised his grade from an F to a C. This experience taught me that the commitment of a single teacher isn't enough: *Everyone must work together for a homework program to succeed, including parents, teachers, coaches, administrators, and students.*

The second problem was with a girl who liked staying after school because it was too noisy and chaotic in her home to study. Her grades had been failing from the beginning of the semester, and I had assumed that she just wasn't very bright. I made arrangements for her to go to the library after school. This arrangement was probably more for my convenience than hers, but proved workable. Her grades improved dramatically. This experience served as a potent reminder that *there are often simple solutions to what may seem, at first glance, to be very difficult or even insurmountable problems.*

The third problem was with a student who preferred staying in my room to going to basketball practice. He wanted to quit basketball, but his parents wouldn't let him. Since students who failed a class were automatically disqualified from the team, he had decided to fail my class as a route to extricating himself from the sports program. Then, after I'd instituted the new rules, he decided he'd rather spend his time after school in my room than practice with the team. To enable my student to pass my class (and to enable me to go home after school), I spoke to the coach, who willingly agreed to find an excuse to dismiss him from the team. Over the years I was to discover time and time again that homework troubles often mask other problems. *By exploring and resolving homework dilemmas, other problems often come into sharper focus so that they, too, may be resolved.*

In two weeks, I saw even the poorest students develop marvelous study skills, as they struggled to pass my homework assignments, unannounced quizzes, and tests on the first try. Timid students began asking questions when they didn't understand something. When I provided class time for students to begin their homework, even the rowdier students used the time as I intended. Everyone wanted to start on homework while I was there to help them. Those who encountered difficulties while completing assignments at home sought me out before school the next morning, clustered around my desk before the bell rang to ask for explanations, or caught up with me between classes to solicit help. Many students exchanged telephone numbers and called each other in the evening to get and give help. Study groups were spontaneously formed. I did stay after school from time to time to provide additional tutoring and was surprised to find how my own attitude had changed about staying late. Working with such a motivated group had become a pleasure, and I didn't feel resentful about donating extra time to students who I knew were really trying.

An unexpected benefit of my new policies was that my strengths and weaknesses as a teacher were brought into sharper focus. When my lectures or explanations were unclear, the students kept asking questions until they understood. When I talked, everyone listened, so if I hadn't prepared lesson plans adequately or didn't understand some of the material myself, my deficiencies were noticed. If my tests were too hard or poorly written, if my homework assignments were exceptionally difficult or lengthy, students received failing grades and I had to suffer the consequences and stay after school along with them. We were really all in this together, and a true spirit of cooperation developed. As they became better students, they forced me to be a better teacher.

My teaching experiences taught me that the formula for solving most homework problems involved combining a stable structure so that students knew where they stood, flexibility to ensure that individual needs were met, and a willingness to let students teach me a few things.

In the past eleven years my work as a private practice psychologist has brought me into contact with countless other children whose school problems were caused or aggravated by their refusal to study. As I listen to the various motivational techniques parents employ to try to get their children to do homework, I realize that their repertoire is often a repeat or extension of the techniques my parents used on my brother Bill a quarter of a century ago. Modern parents lecture, plead, argue, ground, revoke privileges, spank, bribe, and do much of the homework themselves. Yet nothing works for more than a few weeks. Homework skirmishes are fought by thousands of parents every school night. All too often the children end up winning the battle, which means that in the end they have really lost the war.

Finally I advised one family to try my technique. I asked them to set up a regular study time, ensure the house was free from distractions, insist the child remain seated for an hour each evening, and then leave the child alone! The parents shook their heads doubtfully. "It sounds too simple," they said, echoing my parents' sentiments. I assured them that simplicity was the beauty of the technique. Since I was the psychologist, the parents agreed to give it a try.

It took several weeks to iron out that child's manipulations and attempts to thwart the program. And it took me several years to refine my method to overcome the manipulations countless other children employed in their efforts to avoid studying. There are only two remaining avenues children have taken to undermine this program: I haven't found a way to help children who run away from home to avoid doing their homework. And I haven't found a solution for children who become physically violent when told their study period is beginning. For these children, I recommend professional therapy.

Philosophy

The philosophy of this homework program requires parents to adhere to several basic beliefs listed below. Parents should consider whether or not they can accept the following value statements long enough to get their child established on the homework program:

■ **You can lead a horse to water, but you can't make him drink!** In other words, parents can set up conditions so conducive to studying it would be hard for the child to resist using the study time productively, but the bottom line is that the child is the one to exercise the ultimate choice to study or not study. (Don't be alarmed — most non-studiers do use their study time appropriately within short order.)

This can be a difficult value for some parents to adopt. Adults who foresee the long-term repercussions of not doing homework may find it painful to acknowledge their inability to control their child in this area. Adults who cannot tolerate feelings of helplessness and powerlessness may find it especially hard to admit their inability to control others, especially when the "others" are their own children.

The hardest part of being a parent is having to stand at a distance and watch children make choices which may hurt them in the long run. It is natural to try to protect them from harm. Yet, sometimes protectiveness backfires, serving only to protect them from the reality of life. Instead of helping, loved ones may be robbed of the chance to learn from their own mistakes. Yet sometimes that is the way people must learn.

In spite of rapid technological developments, there are still no remote control devices on the market that work for children. Parents can set up idyllic conditions and generous rewards to encourage studying and learning; whether or not children avail themselves of the opportunities is up to them.

This program teaches parents to set firm limits regarding homework and studying. It helps parents and children form a partnership so the child is less inclined to expend time and energy engaging in power struggles. At best, the partnership is a productive one. At least, it is a healthy one.

■ **If it doesn't work, fix it!** The second value statement implies that parents recognize that the methods they used in the past have not worked and are willing to try something new. By beginning this program, parents are making a firm commitment to take corrective action and continue to seek solutions until homework problems are resolved.

■ **If it works, don't fix it!** This third value statement acknowledges that children who are already responsible students do not require the strict structure provided by this program. Parents need not implement all of the procedures discussed to accomplish their goals. If parents have found other techniques that motivate a problem studier, they should certainly feel free to incorporate them into this program.

■ **If at first you don't succeed, try, try again!** The fourth value statement implies a need for consistency. While it is impossible for parents to be totally consistent (some days they simply lack the energy to cope), they do need to make heroic efforts to be consistent during the first ten days the child is on the program. If parents are unable to follow the program for a two-week period, they are to apologize for the interruption and set a date to begin again. It is unrealistic to expect continued attention to homework on the part of the child, if parents cannot be consistent in implementing the program.

Theory

The psychological theories underlying this approach to solving homework problems are behavioral—as in doing whatever it takes to get your child to behave! In actuality, four major theories were drawn upon in formulating the final program: learning theory, humanistic theory, systems theory, and behavior modification.

■ **Learning theory** emphasizes that children are not born knowing how to organize themselves or their environment (although most parents have found children to be extremely adept at disorganizing it!). Parents or caregivers must supply sufficient structure, limits, and controls for the child to function productively. When such external factors are consistently provided by a loving caretaker, children will internalize the controls, thereby developing the ability to create their own structure. *Teaching children to structure and organize forms the basis of this program.*

The concept of logical consequences is used extensively in this program. Although children receive extensive guidance from parents, they are allowed to experience the consequences of their own behavior throughout this program.

■ **Humanistic theory** emphasizes that children's feelings are important determinants of behavior. As parents institute elements of this program that focus on behavior, they are asked to be considerate of their child's feelings. To this end, it is important that they refrain from criticizing, arguing, or making statements which might damage a child's self-esteem or increase his defensiveness.

■ **Systems theory** stresses that if a behavior is to be altered, the entire system that supported the behavior must be altered for changes to endure. This means that if the child is to change, the entire family must change, too. Parents who discover their child is reverting back to past behavior patterns after phasing out of this homework program may need to thoroughly investigate the family dynamics outlined in the next chapter. Sometimes parents unwittingly support their children's poor study habits.

At times, parents must strive to bring about changes on the part of the school. Just as family problems may lead to school problems, so do policies and events at school affect children's motivation and ability to do homework.

Systems theory also states that as one part of a system changes, the other parts of the system are forced to change as well. Indeed, when children's homework is no longer a nightly struggle, the entire family is affected. At times the changes can be unsettling. "Now that he's doing homework so well on his own, I kind of miss the days when he needed me standing over him to do his work," one parent said. "It was a pain, but it also formed the basis of a lot of our time together."

■ **Behavior modification** uses positive reinforcement to reward the child for engaging in a particular behavior, thus causing a repetition of the behavior. Undesirable behaviors are reduced or extinguished by withholding reinforcement. Punishment also leads to a reduction in unwanted behaviors, but frequently increases aggressiveness. Therefore, it is not used in this program.

Most parents have already resorted to punishing non-studiers and have found it doesn't bring about lasting change. Even positive reinforcement doesn't have a lasting effect since many children would rather forego even tempting rewards than do homework. Another behavioral technique, modeling, is a very potent form of teaching which is emphasized throughout this program. Children are more likely to do what parents do than what parents tell them to do. Parents are asked to serve as role models to demonstrate by their deeds, rather than just with their words, exactly how important they think homework really is.

He/She...Hers/His...Himself/Herself

Given the tendency of girls to be more compliant and rule-bound, there are probably more males than females who are resistant to doing homework. However, my tendency to use masculine pronouns throughout this book is in no way meant to indicate that I see boys' problems as more important or serious. It is merely a reflection of my discomfort with the semantic difficulties of acknowledging both sexes. Please forgive me for taking the easy way out of the himself/herself dilemma. Female students are equally in my heart, if not in my vocabulary.

Chapter 2

Dynamics:
School,
Family,
Student

Parents want their children to get a good education.

Teachers want students to learn.

Youngsters want to please their parents and teachers, and to learn.

It would seem logical for homework to serve as a point of contact between parents, teachers, and students, as they strive to achieve their mutual objectives. Yet, all too often, homework becomes the focal point of their individual frustrations, serving instead to divide them.

Why do these natural allies find it hard to join forces to accomplish their goals?

Many parents and teachers are mystified by the difficulties in motivating students to accept responsibility for their studies. "When I was growing up, children did their homework when they were told," they say. "Why won't my children listen when told to do theirs?"

Yet when asked to recall their own childhood experiences, few adults relate memories of having enjoyed homework. "I just did it," most say. When pressed to recall their feelings at the time, even those who liked school acknowledge they didn't care much for doing assignments in the evenings. They preferred to play or pursue other activities. What motivated them to do their school work? Most with whom I have talked cite their desire to please or the fear of displeasing their own parents and teachers as having formed the basis of their compliance. Does this mean today's children are unconcerned about pleasing and do not fear being punished?

While I have seen no evidence to indicate that children's desire to please the adults in their world differs, societal changes have dramatically altered the nature of parent-child and teacher-child relationships. Examining the changes helps clarify the problems parents and educators face in motivating today's students.

Societal Changes

The authoritarian structure of households which was prevalent prior to World War II, crumbled soon afterwards. In part, this was due to women having served as heads-of-household during the war. Husbands and wives began relating to one another on a more egalitarian footing, and families developed a democratic orientation. In the process, children developed a new concept of authority. Rather than seeing mother comply with father's demands as in autocratic homes of the past, they heard her question his authority and speak her own mind. As more and more household decisions were made by a team effort, children learned there is no absolute authority that must be obeyed. Parents who were not strongly united found it required more effort to get children to comply with family rules.

Permissive child-rearing methods, which came into vogue in the 1950s and continued through the 1960s, further altered the nature of parent-child and teacher-student relationships. In the permissive approach, parents believed in allowing children to follow their own inclinations when possible and provided more opportunities for decision-making. Rather than placing youngsters on regimented schedules, parents considered and responded to the individual child's needs.

As parents became more flexible and child-centered, youngsters learned that rules might be altered to take their particular needs into account. As parents came to view youngsters as people in their own right, they permitted increased opportunities for self-expression. Parents were more receptive to hearing children's opinions, discussing issues, and negotiating agreements. Old notions about "sparing the rod and spoiling the child" and "laying down the law" were viewed as potentially damaging to developing personalities.

When children were allowed to communicate their feelings and provide input in establishing family rules, parents found themselves confronting a major dilemma. Enforcing rules over their children's stated objections placed parents in an adversarial role, which was contrary to the parental goal to serve as a loving guide. Forcing compliance caused parents to feel they were employing authoritarian methods that they did not believe in or consider healthy for children.

Changing Lifestyles

Enforcing rules to set limits on children's behaviors is one of the more draining aspects of parenting. The many changes in lifestyle during the past thirty years have combined to create a tremendous drain on the time and energy of family members, leaving them tired, if not exhausted, much of the time. Finding ways to reduce stress and combat it's ill effects has remained a national preoccupation for the last two decades.

The continued erosion of the extended family has forced more and more families to function without the emotional support and concrete assistance a network of relatives once provided. Families who have followed jobs to distant cities or states must function without a network of friends to turn to for support and assistance for the year or two it takes them to become established in a new community. Parents have become increasingly isolated, tending to their children's needs and managing family problems with little external support.

As women joined the work force en masse beginning in the 1960s, increasing numbers of youngsters spent time living in households where both parents worked. Improved economic conditions, the changed role of women, and lack of a support system placed new stresses on marriages. Divorce became an increasingly viable option, and the divorce rate skyrocketed during the 1970s and 1980s, as did the number of children spending time in single parent homes.

When a working parent or parents return home at the end of the day, most have only a few meager hours between the time they get home from work and the children's bedtime. Those hours must be spent cooking, overseeing baths, and tending to a myriad of other chores. Working parents often find the necessity of balancing job and household, and attending to their children's physical and emotional needs exhausting and stressful.

Even traditional families in which one parent works and the other stays home operate at a much more hectic pace than in the past. In families where one spouse travels much of the time or works evenings, the parent who stays at home is often overwhelmed. "Even though I'm married, I feel like a single parent," many say. "I have to manage the children and the household alone much of the time."

Meanwhile, many parents in traditional families find themselves trying to fill the void created by the large number of single parents and dual-income households. "There's another kind of 'single' parent few people think about," one mother told me. "I'm the only parent on the block who is home during the day. I'm listed as the emergency contact at school for five other children whose parents work. The UPS driver rings my doorbell all day long asking me to accept packages for working neighbors. I can't find other parents to share in a car pool. Neighborhood children who are home alone after school come to our house to play; I can't let my children visit them since there is no adult to supervise. I am constantly called upon to volunteer at school because no one else is available. I, too, have a hard time devoting time and energy to my kids' homework."

The altered face of the family has increased the stresses to which children are subjected. Family mobility means that youngsters lack the nurturing and support grandparents, uncles, aunts, nieces and nephews afforded to previous generations. Children whose parents divorce must endure the trauma of separation from a parent. Their financial status is likely to decline, and increasing numbers live at or below the poverty level. If a parent remarries, children must negotiate new relationships with step-parents, stepsiblings, and half-siblings.

Growing up in a single parent home or in a family in which both parents work often means the child leaves home at 7:00 a.m. to go to a day-care center or baby-sitter and does not return home until 6:30 at night. Latchkey children — youngsters who go home after school while their parent or parents are still at work — must fend for themselves without adult supervision for several hours each day. Many are expected to do household chores and school assignments before parents get home, so the family can spend some relaxed time together in the evenings. While this seems a logical way to relieve a crowded family timetable, it means that many youngsters must function independently and autonomously.

To provide added protection for latchkey children, many parents insist they stay in the house until a parent returns from work. Being confined at home means they get less exercise, have less time to interact with friends, and spend more time viewing television. Today, the majority of children are being raised in homes where both parents work. Most will spend some time in a single-parent home before age 18.

Teachers often believe changed lifestyles and permissive child-rearing methods are to blame for the increasingly serious and prevalent academic and behavioral problems they note among students. It is true that modern lifestyles place tremendous stresses both on parents and children. However, few parents still subscribe to the permissive approach. In the 1970s and 1980s, parents began to employ child-rearing methods which attended to children's conduct. The use of behavior modification techniques, which involved rewarding desired behaviors and ignoring undesirable ones, came into vogue. Child psychologists, emphasizing children's needs for structure and limits, developed large followings. Parents continued to try to avoid punitive methods, employing positive approaches to discipline by offering limited choices, developing consequences for unacceptable behavior, and praising good conduct. At the same time, parents continued to encourage children to talk about their feelings.

A Collective Case of the "Guilties"

When parents are chronically tired and stressed, they find it difficult to respond with the consistency necessary for positive discipline methods to succeed. When they are worried about basic issues concerning their children's welfare, it is harder to respond with the requisite firmness these methods require. And most modern parents are not only tired and stressed, but also very worried about the effects of modern lifestyles on their youngsters. Adults who have chosen major changes to improve their personal well-being may labor under feelings of anxiety and guilt as well.

A decision to relocate to pursue a better job may secure or improve the family's financial well-being, but parents worry about the instability such an uprooting creates for youngsters leaving friends and relatives behind. Parents who divorce worry about whether their youngsters will bear emotional scars. Single parents feel inadequate to meet all their children's physical and emotional needs. Parents who remarry worry about the tremendous adjustment children must make to living with new family members. Working parents worry about the adequacy of care provided at day-care centers and by baby-sitters, or the lack of supervision, if children are alone at home. They have concerns about the long-term consequences of their own reduced role in their children's lives. Other parents worry about the indirect effects these lifestyles have on their children: they note increased expressions of insecurity on the part of their own children when a friend's parents separate, move, or have financial problems that require both parents to work.

Parents who fear their youngsters are suffering deprivations may consciously or unconsciously strive to make restitution. Often this takes the form of being more sensitive to their youngster's unhappiness, and having a harder time enforcing compliance with rules and limits. As one parent said, "My kids have been through so much, and I have so little time to be with them given my work schedule. I don't like to spend our precious time together nagging them about homework or policing their studies."

The result is that many parents have adopted a "crisis management" approach to child-rearing and to issues such as homework.

1 The parent communicates expectations as to what constitutes proper behavior. (For example, the youngster is told that he is to do his homework regularly and to the best of his ability.)

2 Parental exhaustion and time constraints preclude consistent attention to working with the child to improve behavior. (The parent doesn't monitor and supervise homework on a daily basis.)

3 Parental worries, anxiety, and guilt prevent following through with limits. (The parent responds to the child's anger about having to study by allowing him to put off or avoid the work, or by doing some of it for him.)

4 When a crisis arises, the parent intervenes. (When the child's grades decline or teachers signal a problem with the child's homework, the parent reprimands the child, reiterates expectations, and sets firmer limits.)

5 The child is made to feel guilty but he still lacks the maturity, skills, and self-discipline to change his behavior. (The child is sorry, promises to do better, but lacks the wherewithal to do homework responsibly.)

6 The parent's exhaustion and worries prevent a sustained response, and the problems eventually repeat themselves. (The parent does not focus on homework problems until they are solved, and the problems eventually recur.)

Thus, parents become involved at times of "crisis," try to take action, but are unable to sustain an effort long enough to solve the problem.

Family Dynamics

Just as societal trends affect the way families approach and deal with homework, trends within a family affect the way children approach and deal with studying. Children are highly responsive to family dynamics. Sensitive children may react to subtle themes and underlying messages despite their inability to discuss or even consciously comprehend what is transpiring. Because most children dislike homework to begin with and because educational endeavors absorb so much of their time, studying frequently becomes the arena in which family problems are acted out.

The dynamics discussed below demonstrate how troubled family relationships impact on homework. However, it is important to remember that homework difficulties can and do develop in normal, everyday families! *Homework problems do not necessarily reflect deep-seated problems in family relationships or among individual family members!* Just as it is important for parents to be alert to family dynamics which may aggravate homework and study problems, it is important to remember that homework problems are so widespread that they occur in almost every family at one time or another.

■ **"Let me fix it."** Some children discover that homework problems serve to reduce or mitigate other family tensions. Many marriages are fraught with discord, yet when there is a problem regarding a child, some parents form an alliance to resolve it.

Children who are distressed by parental conflict may strive to "fix the marriage" and unite parents by developing academic problems. Even if the parents' response is to reprimand youngsters, many prefer to be scolded than to hear parents argue. It is as though such children are saying, "Be mad at me if you must; just don't be mad at one another!" In fact, many parents have told me they would like to get a divorce, but need to stay together to help a troubled child. Similarly, I have known children who experience considerable distress over the way a sibling is treated by a parent. They act out to draw parental wrath away from the scapegoated sibling.

■ **"I'll take any kind of attention I can get."** It is a truism that negative attention is better than no attention at all. Most children would rather be scolded or even punished than ignored. Parents who do not satisfy their children's needs for affection may respond when they misbehave, withdrawing after correcting the problematic behavior. Such attention provides reinforcement for misbehavior. Further, parents may equate punishment with affection by saying, "I'm doing this because I love you," when scolding or spanking. This encourages some children to misbehave to obtain reassurance of the parents' love.

■ **Getting mad—getting even.** How can a child express anger towards parents? If parents value education and have a fervent desire for their youngster to achieve academically, one guaranteed method is to deal a blow to the parents' value system. The more upset parents become when the child ignores school responsibilities, the better this method serves as a vehicle for expressing angry feelings. This dynamic appears most often in families in which children are not permitted to express their angry feelings directly.

■ **"I'll never be as successful as you are."** Although some parents say they want their child to succeed, they experience unconscious conflicts about the youngster's success. Many parents compete with their child. Some are afraid of losing their youngster's admiration or respect if the child surpasses them. When a child is studying to be a brain surgeon while mother is "only" a nurse or father is "only" a medical technician, pride in and resentment over a child's accomplishments can coexist simultaneously. Envious parents may actually discourage their youngster by belittling his academic successes; loving children may comply by failing to fulfill their potential.

While children may not have the words to verbalize their awareness of this dynamic, they see their parents become upset or even angry when they do well, and are often quite aware of what is happening. When these children set themselves up for failure by not doing their homework, it is as if they are saying, "Don't worry, mom and dad, I'll never be better than you."

■ **A chance to do it again.** Many parents displace their anger over their own lack of educational opportunities onto their children. Rather than dealing with their resentment about their own deprivation, they try to work it out through their children. Such parental attitudes are revealed in statements like, "I could have accomplished much more if these opportunities had been available to me."

Although the child is expected to utilize his educational opportunities, he senses that the parent is actually involved in a struggle that does not involve him or his life at all. The resentment this engenders prompts many children to do poorly. "Dad keeps telling me he wants me to do well, but it doesn't seem like he thinks about me or my welfare."

■ **"Somebody's going to make it; I choose you."** While some parents have a hard time coping with their children's successes, others cannot cope with a child's limited abilities. A parent's heart-felt desire may be for one or more of her youngsters to graduate from high school, go to college, or graduate from an Ivy League school. Or, a parent may be bound and determined that her child will carry on a family tradition and prepare for a career the parent has selected.

Youngsters experience such pressures as overwhelming, if they lack the ability to achieve at levels commensurate with parental expectations. Adolescents are likely to rebel, if their personal interests and aspirations are at odds with their parents' plans for their future. These children may say, "Now that I've flunked so many science classes, will you let me go to the conservatory and major in art, instead of majoring in science in college?"

■ **"I'm not you."** Some parents view their children as extensions of themselves. The confrontation with the realities of their youngster's unique strengths and weaknesses undermines their feelings of closeness. "If she cared about me, she'd do well in history. I'm a history major," one father said of his daughter. "I think she's doing poorly just to spite me." In some cases the parents are correct: Children may reject the parent's favored subject to establish more emotional distance and retain a sense of self by asserting their separate identity.

■ **"Please love me for me."** Many children respond to parental pressure to perform academically by becoming underachievers. Sometimes it is a way of expressing anger and of "getting even." Often students who cannot live up to parental expectations become discouraged and give up.

At other times, doing poorly in the face of pressure to perform is a non-verbal plea for affirmation. "Please love me for who I am — not for my good grades." Teenagers are particularly prone to react to this dynamic, especially if they doubt that their parents truly care about them. If many conflicts over identity issues such as clothing, hairstyles, music, and friends are occurring, adolescents may become increasingly bent on a course of academic self-destruction in hopes of receiving parental affirmation. "If they cared, they'd love and accept me for who I am. It wouldn't matter how I do in school," they say.

■ **"I'm too depressed to study."** Going to school and studying is like a job for children. Just as adults have a hard time finding the energy to concentrate and work productively when they are depressed, the same is true of children. Depression is probably the most misdiagnosed illness of childhood. Children who are clinically depressed are often considered to be merely going through "a phase." Few adults stop to consider what "a phase" really means.

"He used to be good about doing homework. Suddenly it became a struggle," says parent after parent. "I thought it was just a stage, but he didn't snap out of it, and now his grades have been affected."

Common family stresses which precipitate depression in children include: parental divorce, the birth of a younger sibling, an older sibling leaving home, a family move, parental unemployment, or living with another family member who is depressed, drug addicted, or alcoholic.

Individual problems a child is experiencing may precipitate depression: not making a sports team, not achieving an honor or award, the death of a pet, being unpopular, the loss of an important friend. Unless parents can find a way to help youngsters resolve such personal problems, their school work is likely to be affected.

■ **"I'm too handicapped to study."** Parents of a child who suffers from any sort of physical, emotional, or educational handicap may have a hard time being firm about their child's need to study. Children learn that if they say, "I'm too sick," "It hurts too much," or "It's too hard for me," they can cut their study session short, get parents to do some of the work, or get them to write an excuse.

Psychosomatic illnesses can pose special problems. On the one hand, the child is truly too ill to study. On the other hand, excusing him from studying supports the effectiveness of illness as a coping mechanism.

■ **"Don't worry, I'll never grow up."** Some parents derive their sense of self and reason for being from their children. Having a youngster who depends on them builds their self-esteem and provides a sense of purpose. These parents may pamper a child (typically the last born), discouraging the development of autonomous behaviors that support independent functioning. They may take over when the child finds things difficult or redo his work. Although the overt message to the child may be, "I want you to do well," the covert message may be, "I need you to need me."

Youngsters may continue to do poorly or fail despite vast amounts of parental tutoring and teaching as if to say, "Don't worry, I'll never graduate, grow up, and leave you."

■ **"Help me, I'm drowning!"** When children are upset and aren't able to talk about their problems, they may do something guaranteed to draw attention to themselves, such as flagrantly mishandling their responsibilities. School and homework problems may sound an alarm loud enough for parents to hear. Indeed, many adults who are oblivious to their child's emotional problems become concerned when academic performance wanes. Some parents first learn of their child's substance abuse problem when investigating deteriorating grades or other school problems. They didn't hear the slurred speech, smell the alcohol on his breath, or notice the stumbling gait. They do notice poor report card grades.

■ **"Help Dad, he's drowning!"** When children who have been doing well in school suddenly develop academic problems, it is common for teachers to notice. Youngsters who are troubled by serious family problems such as alcoholism, a suicidal parent, family violence, or a parent's health may develop school problems as a way to draw attention to their plight. It is common for these students to stop doing homework, but to continue to function well at school as if to say, "The problem is at home, not at school." This dynamic is so common that when a youngster is referred for mental health services, he is designated as the "identified patient" rather than simply "the patient" to acknowledge his status as the one who got help for the "unidentified patients" in his family.

■ **"I'm just like dear old Dad."** Children who closely identify with a parent may emulate him or her. Just as parents accentuate similarities between themselves and their children as a way to feel closer, so, too, many children say, "I have trouble with math, just like Dad." When a parent and child are emotionally fused, the pressure to be "just the same" is very intense. These parents often smile when discussing their child's academic problems and make comments like, "He's just a chip off the old block. I didn't do homework when I was a child, either." Similarly, a student may become a compulsive overachiever hoping to do well in a parent's favored subject.

A few parents have even suggested that the similarities with their child are genetic. "I didn't do my studies when I was growing up. Neither does my child. I think he inherited it from me." Genes do not control homework-doing. However, parents who were not taught the skills and attitudes needed for effective studying find it hard to teach their children. Homework problems are often an intergenerational affair.

Dynamics of Homework

Students have similar reactions to homework and studying despite their vast individual differences. This is because the dynamics of the educational process, of parental reactions to homework problems, and of being a student impact children in similar ways. Understanding these dynamics provides a framework for examining and altering homework problems.

Educational Dynamics

Most schools follow the factory model of education, attempting to produce "finished products" in assembly-line fashion. The raw materials, young children, are harvested from home at age six and transported to schools for processing, regardless of their maturity. Educators attempt to install new skills and competencies before advancing students to the next grade. In the majority of institutions, the pace cannot be significantly altered to account for individual differences, since the deadline for delivering the product to market is inflexible: Students must be ready to graduate in about twelve years. Therefore, a pace must be maintained that bores some students while making it impossible for others to keep up. There are few attractive alternatives for students who require much less or much more time to complete their education, so they are usually considered "problems," much like defective parts.

The pressure placed upon students in this kind of environment is tremendous, so it is understandable that many become emotional drop-outs whether or not they actually physically withdraw from school before graduation. Yet to alter this dynamic would require:

1 Creating educational programs which are completely individualized, to account for different student interests, abilities and learning styles

2 Providing self-paced programs that afford students as much or as little time as they need to learn material

3 Matching individual students and teachers according to learning style and personality type to create the best possible learning environment for each child.

Instituting these reforms would take years of transition. Although it is very important to continue to work toward educational change, altering the dynamics of parent-child interactions is a more manageable goal for families facing immediate problems.

Dynamics of Parents

Parents whose children have difficulties with homework experience similar pressures and problems, and tend to react in similar ways.

■ **Fears of failure.** Most parents know that children mature and learn at different rates, and that some simply require more time to learn than others. However, society in general and the structure of our educational system in particular cause most parents to develop intense anxiety about the speed at which their child learns.

Our society typically equates rate of learning with intellect and success. The student who graduates from high school at age 16 is much admired for his genius, while the one who graduates at age 20 is pitied for being intellectually slow. It matters not that both students have mastered the same material, much less that the 16-year-old may be tense, driven, unhappy, and socially maladjusted while the 20-year-old may be relaxed, happy, and has many friends. Assumptions about the relationship between speed of learning and success persist, even though many precocious youngsters accomplish little of note during their adult years, while many whose poor achievement prompted them to withdraw from high school eventually attain advanced college degrees later in life...and use them!

The design of schools forces parents to be as concerned with the *speed* at which their child matures and masters skills as with *whether* he matures or masters skills. Most parents strive to communicate the importance of speed to their children:

"Hurry up and get started," parents may say when it is time for the child to study.

"What's taking you so long?" they may ask when a child has spent a long time completing a few problems. Rarely is it a straightforward inquiry. More often parents sound concerned or irritated, communicating that it is undesirable to take a long time. Indeed, a child who works slowly is likely to have problems in school, regardless of his intelligence.

"Quit being lazy!" parents may say to a child who has a different concept of time or takes a more relaxed approach to learning. Children who have a different concept of time will not do well on the many timed tests at school where speed is a factor. Those who take a relaxed approach to learning often fall behind and cannot catch up. Schools impose relentless deadlines for learning.

"If you don't learn your school lessons tonight, you'll fail your test tomorrow!" parents admonish. They may communicate that there are no second chances — once the moment for learning something has passed, it is gone forever. Unfortunately, the design of classrooms is such that this is often true.

"If you don't keep up with your assignments, you'll fail sixth grade," parents warn their youngster. Yet, failing a grade usually means the child needs more time to learn. What parents are really warning is, "If you don't keep up, you'll need more time to learn!" Yet, few parents could bring themselves to say, "If you don't learn your school lessons this year, you will have to learn them next year." The child just might decide to wait until next year, or the year after that. Given the nature of our society and our school system, that would signify real failure.

This same dynamic encourages the development of compulsive study habits, causing many students to run a race against the invisible clock, cramming in every bit of knowledge they can. The dilemma for parents is that these compulsive children are admired. Parents who confide their concerns about their "perfect" students to others may be viewed as having convoluted goals for their youngsters.

■ **Secrecy.** Parents who find it difficult to motivate their youngsters to study are inclined to keep their plight to themselves, as though guarding a shameful secret. Although homework problems are so widespread as to touch almost every household, many parents are hesitant to admit to difficulties managing this supposedly simple and basic aspect of child-rearing. It is as though they are convinced every other child in every other household is calmly saying, "Now that dinner is over, I'll go right to my room and do my homework. I'll do it all by myself, without any help from you unless I really get stuck. I'll check my work when I'm done. Then I'll read the book for the report that's due in two weeks. I'll be finished in plenty of time to get ready for bed."

This is, of course, an exaggeration. Few parents are so naive as to believe every other child responds like the one above. At the same time, they have a hard time believing most of their neighbors confront their own homework dilemmas, even such pillars of the community as PTA presidents, second grade school teachers, and parents of students on the high school math team. Many find it difficult to comprehend that highly educated parents and parents of brilliant students find their background to be relatively useless when dealing with a recalcitrant 8-year-old — not to mention an unmotivated 12-year-old or rebellious adolescent.

■ **Feelings of insecurity.** When a parent receives a note from school saying, "Johnny hasn't been doing his geography assignments. Please make sure he gets them done," parents often interpret this to mean that they are supposed to know how to motivate the child. Many are hesitant to ask questions that might reveal their lack of knowledge as to how to do this. When parents do phone or go to school to discuss such a request in more detail, they usually receive a more in-depth understanding of their child's problems, but often leave without ideas as to how to solve them. When parents ask how to get their child to accept responsibility for homework, they may be told, "Just tell your child to do the work." Such a response makes parents feel very insecure, since they believe the teacher is saying other children automatically do what parents tell them. It is common for parents to leave such conferences questioning themselves and their personal adequacy.

Sometimes parents receive notes from teachers which contain requests which sound simple and reasonable: "Johnny didn't finish his math in school today. Please have him do it at home." If they try to comply but cannot fulfill the teacher's expectations, parents may not stop to consider that they are being asked to get their child to do something which even the teacher has been unable to do. Doubts about their competence as parents become more troubling. When conscientious parents believe it is their responsibility to see that the work gets done but cannot motivate or succeed at teaching their youngster, many know of only one solution: to do it themselves! These conscientious parents begin "helping" their children at home and eventually end up doing some of the work for them.

The feelings of inadequacy parents experience when their child is having homework and school problems further lessens the chances that they will risk exposing their dilemma to others. They may feel angry over pressures to assume so much responsibility for their child's education at home and begin to doubt the teacher's competence.

■ **Fears of being judged.** Conscientious parents know that children do better when parents are actively involved in the educational process. Such parents often fear that the reverse is true, also: If their child is acting irresponsibly or having problems at school, they will be judged to be unconcerned parents. Fears of being judged "unconcerned" or "uncaring" place even more pressure on parents.

■ **Worries about the child's education.** As their sense of guilt, shame, failure, and inadequacy is added to fears and worries about the child's educational progress, some parents lose control and become overly harsh and punitive with their youngster. It is frightening to most parents to hear that their child isn't doing well in school. Prospects of having one's own youngster become a school drop-out who is unable to find decent employment and function as a contributing member of society loom large. It is hard for parents to remain calm when they are notified about school problems. Many overreact. The child may respond by becoming increasingly upset and rebellious. To further complicate matters, some children are compliant at home: They learn the school lessons, do assignments, and study. However, many proceed to lose the homework papers, appear unprepared at school the next day, fail tests, or present behavioral problems in class. Parents may become suspicious when teachers continue to report problems they cannot see or comprehend.

■ **Lack of guidance.** When parents ask teachers exactly what they should do to get children to do homework, teachers usually lack ready answers themselves. Most admit to their own frustrations motivating students. They feel overwhelmed by administrative duties, the behavioral problems displayed by increasing numbers of students, and the changes in learning styles and attitudes brought about by societal changes. Although teachers' goals are to ensure that each student learns each lesson, time constraints make this impossible.

When parents press teachers for solutions and receive unclear recommendations or suggestions they do not know how to follow, parents often worry that the child's problems are so serious that even the teacher is overwhelmed by them. In the absence of solid advice, many parents panic. Their attempts to intervene in their child's problems may become increasingly ineffective or even counterproductive.

Student Dynamics

Years ago the phrase "boys will be boys" referred to the fact that normal, active, healthy males preferred to run and jump and play than sit still and do homework. That does not mean they were permitted to forego studying, or that their parents enjoyed struggling to get them to "hit the books." It does mean parents grasped the motivations of boys who employed every trick in the book to avoid homework.

The women's movement has wrought many changes, and now it is common for girls to be less compliant and more active than in the past, too. This may explain why increasing numbers of girls are diagnosed as having behavioral and learning problems. "Children will be children" would be a more appropriate phrase to describe the vast majority of homework problems.

■ **Educational constraints.** Unfortunately, parents and educators often view children's distaste for homework as abnormal. Some cite the fact that little children have a tremendous love of learning and never tire of studying their world. Adults overlook the fact that little ones are free to choose what and when they want to learn: They have the freedom to study a caterpillar that piques their interest, as well as the freedom to pursue another subject when something else catches their eye. Further, the majority of a pre-school child's learning opportunities are experiential.

Even students with wide-ranging interests and an unquenchable thirst for knowledge tire of having to learn about the world second-hand, that is, by reading and being told about it, as is the custom in school. They tire even more quickly if they must sit while doing homework, after having already spent most of the day sitting at school. They tire more quickly still if they are not allowed to pursue topics that pique their interest, but must focus, instead, on material the teacher has selected. Such factors explain why most students dislike most homework assignments.

■ **Personality.** A child's personality type affects not only his overall feelings about homework, but his preferences for particular types of assignments and projects as well. Introverts are more likely to be amenable to closing themselves in with only their books for company than extroverts who are revitalized by social time and find solitary activities more draining. Group projects and class presentations may appeal to extroverts, while introverts may be resistant to assignments and projects requiring group participation. Children who are "thinkers" may enjoy activities involving an objective approach to managing facts and concepts; "feelers" prefer expressive activities that require subjective analysis and judgement. "Sensing" individuals who like practical matters may better tolerate homework assignments emphasizing facts and figures than "intuitives," who are stimulated by more creative endeavors.

Yet a child's individual personality is rarely taken into account when homework is assigned. Most assignments are given to an entire class, and everyone is expected to complete them. The teacher's personality type influences the kinds of assignments he or she develops, and a student with a very different personality type may have a hard time relating to many or even most of the assignments.

■ **Learning styles.** A student with a concrete-sequential learning style who is more organized, task-oriented, and prone to focus on factual details may work better with assignments emphasizing structure and practical, hands-on activities. A concrete-random learning style may incline a student toward open-ended assignments that allow for exploration and experimentation. Abstract-sequential learners prefer working with overall concepts and theories. Those with an abstract-random learning style may do best with assignments allowing an imaginative, flexible, and global approach, emphasizing interpretation and application of concepts.

Again, an individual student's learning style is rarely taken into account when homework assignments are made. This is not necessarily bad, since it encourages students to go beyond their preferred style and function under different sorts of conditions. However, the lack of regard for different learning styles does explain the problems many students have relating to and completing various assignments. A student who receives many assignments utilizing a different learning style may have problems with the homework.

Student Preferences

Differing interests and preferences for certain types of subjects, materials, assignments, and teachers influence a student's approach to homework. Parents and teachers may be mystified by what appears to be a highly sporadic or inconsistent approach to homework on the part of a particular student. If they look more carefully, they are apt to see patterns emerge.

■ **"Daily assignments only, please."** Some children do their daily homework assignments, but avoid less structured long-range assignments such as studying for quizzes and tests, reading a book for a book report, doing a research paper or art project. While their report card grades may not suffer too much in elementary school, children who only complete daily assignments may begin to fail classes in middle school and in high school. These children often have a hard time planning ahead, working independently, or functioning in unstructured situations. They may feel overwhelmed when confronted by big tasks, and have difficulty breaking down large projects into small steps. Some students function best doing daily assignments because they receive more immediate feedback, which helps them stay motivated.

■ **"Long-range projects only, please."** Other children disdain daily assignments, but willingly spend long hours doing special projects. This may be a sign that the child is not being sufficiently challenged at school, as daily assignments are often designed to reinforce material learned during the day. Students who already know their spelling words may balk at being required to write each word ten times to "learn" how to spell them. Students who are creative may resist doing more structured or mundane assignments, enjoying instead, putting energy into projects which typically offer opportunities for individual expression.

■ **"Sorry, I don't do math."** Discriminating youngsters can be highly selective about how they spend their after-school hours. They may exert themselves in particular subjects or on particular projects they like or do well in, but neglect the other assignments. They demonstrate the normal tendency to increase their involvement in activities they enjoy and lessen their involvement in activities they dislike. Unfortunately, this may cause them to make poor progress in selected subjects.

■ **"Favored teachers only, please."** Some children work hard in classes if they like the teacher, but refuse to do work in classes if they dislike the teacher. This is especially common among high school students, but occurs among children at all levels. Inconsistent grades frequently reflect this tendency. Some youngsters receive high grades in science in fifth grade, for instance, because they like the teacher, and receive poor grades in science in sixth grade because they dislike the teacher. When children do poorly because they dislike a teacher, they are often expressing anger and attempting to punish the individual teacher involved. It is not until they are fully mature that they realize their actions backfired: the wrong person ended up being punished.

■ **"I won't study for quizzes."** Even some students who are fairly faithful about completing homework don't study for quizzes. Unless they have a specific homework assignment to complete, they forget to take their book or study materials home. It's as if they have one-track minds that repeat, "Nothing due tomorrow means no homework tonight."

■ **"I won't study for tests."** Still other children prepare for quizzes but not for tests. Usually this stems from feeling overwhelmed by the large amount of material to be reviewed. Children who are poorly organized may be uncertain how to coordinate (or even find) their lecture notes, study sheets, homework problems, and textbooks to conduct a review. Children who are behind in a subject may not study for a test because they have already concluded they won't do well on it. Some children suffer from test anxiety and anticipate failure no matter how much they study. They, too, may believe it is pointless to study.

■ **"I won't study for exams."** Even students who study for tests (which usually only cover a chapter or two) may fall apart when it is time to study for semester exams. In part, this may be due to the importance placed on semester exams, which creates overwhelming pressure and anxiety. The idea that failing one exam can lower the grade for the entire semester can be inherently intimidating and unnerving. This problem may first surface in high school where many students encounter semester exams for the first time. Just as some students feel it is pointless to study for tests, those who lack self-confidence or are poorly organized may believe studying for exams is futile. "How can I study a semester's worth of work in a week?" many ask. They say this even though they have been keeping up with their daily work and making good grades on quizzes and tests throughout the semester.

Such students may not know how to skim material by reading topic sentences and key sections in their texts. Instead, they turn back to page one of their history text, realize they don't recall all the names and dates and places of all the significant people and events, and give up on the spot. They mistakenly believe it is necessary to memorize the entire book to pass the exam.

Other students believe exams are a waste of time. "I already passed the chapter tests to show I've learned the material. Why must I take another test on the same material?" they complain. They may handle their anger by refusing to study.

■ **"I'll only do the easy stuff."** Some children are so insecure and lacking in self-confidence, they will not even attempt items they perceive as difficult. Homework can be an exceptionally painful experience for these children, since facing a homework assignment is like facing their inadequacies. Children with poor tolerance for frustration may go so far as to destroy their work by tearing up their papers when they make an error. Others throw away completed papers rather than turn in assignments they fear are poorly done. It is often hard for parents and teachers to understand that even bright children can feel so incompetent they give up without even trying or refuse to turn in work they have spent time completing. Yet this happens often when students are ashamed of their work.

Some insecure children even manage to convince their parents and teachers they really are incompetent, IQ and achievement scores notwithstanding.

■ **"I'll only do homework if you hold my hand."** There are many reasons children refrain from doing their assignments until a parent or teacher is with them. Some are so lacking in confidence, they need continual support and encouragement. Others have parents who are too busy to provide much attention, yet these same parents will make special efforts to attend to their children's requests for assistance with homework. Still other children are very social and like to have someone with whom they can interact while studying.

Homework can be a lonely business for a child, if he is sent to his room to study. It may feel like a punishment if other family members are interacting while he has been isolated in another part of the house. And it can be completely noxious if a sibling with whom the child is in competition is socializing with parents while he is relegated to his room.

■ **"I don't read."** Children who don't like to read or who have problems reading may resist assignments that emphasize it. These students are likely to have increasing problems getting their homework done as they advance in school, since reading loads become increasingly heavy from middle school on.

Similarly, other students may eschew assignments that involve writing. In earlier grades, this often occurs because the emphasis on penmanship causes children with poor motor control to feel ashamed of their handwriting. In later grades, students are more apt to have concerns about the quality of their thoughts or ability to construct grammatical sentences. Even if such children are forced to do the work, they may refuse to turn in papers they deem "not good enough." They may be seen as "lazy" or uncaring. In fact, they care too much.

■ **"I don't do homework. Period."** Most students are vocal about their distaste for homework of any sort. Even those who are faithful studiers will admit to wishing that when the school day ends, it truly ends. And, of course, some children would prefer not to even have to go to school in the first place.

It has been said that work may be defined as "something we are not inclined to do," whereas fun may be defined as "something we are inclined to do." It makes sense, then, that school assignments are called "homework" rather than "homefun" since it is a rare child who finds it fun to sit down to read and write and study...after spending a day sitting down and reading and writing and studying.

Chapter 3

Grade School through High School: How Homework Problems Change

Certain types of problems are more likely to occur at specific points in students' academic careers. In primary school, youngsters develop attitudes toward homework and learning which influence their approach to academic tasks for years to come. Physical changes and social pressures intensify during middle school years. There is a tendency for students to become distracted from learning tasks, as they become more self-conscious and aware of peer relationships. Pre-adolescents with educational deficiencies, those who are having a harder time with developing interpersonal relationships, and those who have not developed good study skills may flounder despite having made good grades in earlier years.

In high school, students have even larger amounts of homework to contend with. Accumulated academic and study skill deficits place a tremendous strain on many students. At the same time, adolescents are preoccupied with identity issues, members of the opposite sex, and with preparing to move out on their own. Family conflicts intensify as parents struggle to prepare teenagers for adult responsibilities.

The following case studies illustrate how serious the problems can become in some families. If your child's problems seem much less severe than the students in these case studies, so much the better. If the problems seem even worse, do not despair. Help is on the way!

Homework in Elementary School: The Case of Johnny Johnson

I have had many occasions to work with elementary school students who are refusing to do their homework. The story of Mrs. Johnson (not her real name) is typical of mothers who have sought my help.

Mrs. Johnson was the mother of a fifth grade student. She had been struggling with her son, Johnny, over homework for several years. Johnny's achievement test scores were in the average range in all areas. His problems in school had begun during the second grade. "He was having trouble memorizing subtraction facts at the time, so the teacher asked me to work with him at home. It was hard, because I had just started working and didn't get home until quite late, and his father traveled a lot in his job. By the time I picked Johnny up from day-care, we were both tired. Our practice sessions were awful! He took forever to learn the problems. I felt he was either slow or just not trying. I'd get frustrated and end up yelling at him when he made mistakes. He would end up in tears. It was traumatic for both of us."

Mrs. Johnson thought Johnny was doing well in third grade, until his first report card arrived. He received several grades of unsatisfactory. Mrs. Johnson immediately arranged an appointment with the teacher. At the conference, she learned that the poor grades were caused by Johnny's failure to do a number of homework assignments. "Up to that point I didn't even know he had homework, but then I started keeping tabs on him. His teacher sent home his assignments and books with him each day. At first he brought them home, but he wouldn't do the work unless his father or I was standing over him." After a few weeks, Johnny began losing the assignment sheets and "forgetting" his books at school.

As Johnny became more obstinate, Mr. and Mrs. Johnson tried everything they could think of. At the teacher's request, Mrs. Johnson drilled Johnny on his spelling words before his tests, since he wouldn't study on his own. Even though Johnny learned the words during the drills, he often did poorly on his school tests anyway. Mr. Johnson promised him a bicycle for his birthday, if he got a good report card. They grounded him from playing with his friends or watching television whenever he received a zero on a homework paper. When the teacher sent home a note saying he hadn't done even one assignment for an entire week, emphasizing again the importance of seeing to it that Johnny studied regularly, his parents punished him further. Nothing worked for very long.

By fifth grade the situation had degenerated to the point that arguments over homework took up a large part of the Johnsons' time every school night. The parents would often end up doing much of the work for Johnny, either because he appeared unable to do it himself, or because they were too tired to spend time nagging him. (Mr. Johnson specialized in math and science, Mrs. Johnson worked with him on reading, spelling, and social studies. They took turns at health.)

"The situation seems hopeless," Mrs. Johnson concluded, trying to blink back the tears. "We can't hold his hand all the way through high school, much less college."

When I asked Johnny to share his thoughts about the homework problem, he replied by rolling his eyes and stating, "Homework is boring." When I probed further in an attempt to fathom the mysteries of his unconscious, I was finally able to get him to elaborate further. "Homework is boring because it's dumb," he said.

■ **Analysis.** When Johnny began having problems, the teacher immediately asked his parents to work with him at home, without first determining whether this was a viable option. Mr. and Mrs. Johnson did not receive guidance as to how to help him. The outcome of their efforts was not assessed to determine whether it would be important to seek other remedies. The Johnsons did not inform the teacher about the problems they were having fulfilling her requests or solicit advice.

The Johnsons' reaction to the teacher's request is common among parents of elementary school children: In their panic when they discover their child needs special help and in their haste to cooperate and make sure the child learns the material, they overlook the importance of seeking ways to make learning an enjoyable experience. The student may learn, but at the same time develops a strong dislike for working on school work at home.

Inadequate communication between Johnny's teachers and parents and between Johnny and his parents also meant that Mr. and Mrs. Johnson were not informed that he had homework until six weeks after he had begun receiving assignments. When they did find out, they felt angry with their son for not having informed them that he had homework all along. An adversarial relationship quickly developed. In the power struggle that ensued, Johnny acted out his anger by doing poorly on tests for which his parents had prepared him.

The Johnsons didn't know how to teach Johnny to assume the responsibility for his own work. While insisting he be responsible, they ended up assuming more responsibility themselves. They focused their many disciplinary methods on results, assuming he had the requisite study skills to enable him to function responsibly.

The characteristic thread that runs through the stories told by parents of elementary school children is that the children's homework responsibilities have been transferred to the parents over the years. Often teachers inadvertently contribute to this process by sending notes home informing parents about assignments. Sometimes they send homework folders home at the end of the week, asking parents to sign a paper indicating that they have seen their child's work. Parents may interpret these messages to mean, "It's up to you, mom and dad, to make sure the work gets done."

Another common theme in the histories of children with homework problems is that the burden of actually teaching some school lessons is transferred to the parents. If the child is not progressing adequately in school, parents may try to fill in the gap. Although it is the teacher's responsibility to do the teaching, the truth of the matter is that classroom teachers may not have the time or energy to make sure every student learns all the material. Delegating teaching responsibility to parents may seem a logical resolution to this problem. However, many parents are unable to teach their children no matter how well-educated they themselves are, and often the "logical" solution creates more problems than it solves. Parents' relationship with their child or lack of familiarity with teaching methods renders them inadequate to provide effective help.

Many parents vacillate between feeling overwhelmed, guilty and resentful. Although some manage to teach the required material, stressful homework sessions may end up doing more harm than good. Children learn to dislike homework more and more. As conflict becomes more intense, many students become increasingly resistant to learning academic material in school as well.

It is common for the following scenario to develop:

1 A child is having academic problems.

2 Teachers ask the parents to "help."

3 Parents tutor and teach.

4 The child welcomes the help at times, but often resents the parents' attempt to step into the teaching role.

5 Parents feel angry with the child who is not appreciative of their efforts. They begin to resent teachers, who they believe are shirking their responsibilities. However, they want to help their child, do not want to be seen as "bad parents," and do not want to alienate the teacher, so they continue to help as best they can.

6 Despite the parents' attempt to remain supportive of the teachers and follow their recommendations, most children realize their parents are frustrated.

7 When children realize their parents disapprove of the teacher's actions, the children's respect for the teacher's authority is further undermined. The child has a tool for manipulating the parents: "Let's all blame the teacher."

8 Teachers become increasingly hostile toward the parents, whom they see as "nonsupportive" and "uncooperative," and come to see parents as the weak link in the educational process.

Thus, problems in the teacher/student relationship affect parent/child and parent/teacher relationships. As relationships deteriorate, students' school and homework problems intensify.

Homework in Middle School: The Case of Jake Smith

Jake Smith's problems didn't come to his parents' attention until the sixth grade. In previous years, Jake had done an adequate job in school. By paying attention in class and making an occasional, half-hearted stab at doing daily and long-range assignments, he had managed to get average grades. Since his achievement and school performance were average, his father, teachers, and Jake, himself, thought he was "just average." Although his mother secretly suspected he was capable of more, Mrs. Smith kept her thoughts to herself, because his test scores and daily work seemed to indicate she was wrong. "After all," she told herself, "I'm sure all mothers like to think their children are brighter than they really are."

In sixth grade Jake stopped paying attention in class. That is, he stopped paying attention to the teacher. He paid lots of attention to the other boys, and occasionally to the girls as well. Since he had always been quiet and withdrawn, Mr. and Mrs. Smith had often hoped he would "come out of his shell" and make more friends. Now, in sixth grade, they began to wish he would crawl back inside!

Jake's grades fell from mostly C's to several D's and one F. Mr. and Mrs. Smith were very upset, but Jake seemed unconcerned. "It's no big deal," was his only reply when they tried to talk to him about the problem.

Jake had to attend summer school after sixth grade to make up the math class he had failed, and this was upsetting to him. Mr. and Mrs. Smith hoped forfeiting part of his summer vacation might teach him a lesson. Unfortunately, Jake didn't learn it. During the summer, Jake solidified friendships with a few other students with academic problems who shared his dislike of school.

Jake did pass summer school. However, after the fourth week of seventh grade, two of Jake's teachers sent notes home stating Jake was in danger of failing. Jake insisted that the notes were "no big deal"; he would still pass the quarter. Mr. and Mrs. Smith wanted to believe their son. To demonstrate their trust, they limited their response to asking Jake every night if he had homework. If he admitted that he did, they sent him to his room to study. If he denied having homework, they interrogated him and sometimes sent him to his room to study or read, anyway. They expressed their concerns about his friends, since they could see he was identifying with a troubled peer group. Jake's response was to become rebellious and defiant.

In spite of the Smiths' attempts to motivate Jake to pay attention in class, to get extra help, and to do his homework, Jake continued to "do his own thing" at school. "His thing" consisted of writing notes to his friends during class, visiting their homes in the early evening, and talking to them on the phone. During a particularly heated exchange that occurred after his parents learned he would definitely fail seventh grade, Jake shouted, "Do you want me to be an egghead or something? Nobody does well in school! And I wouldn't be caught dead in the special education class, either. It just isn't cool!"

That was when Mr. and Mrs. Smith realized an important truth about Jake's school problems: His peer standing and social life were more important to him than academic success.

■ **Analysis.** In several respects, Jake Smith's story is typical of children whose academic problems first surface during sixth, seventh, and eighth grades. *Many children who have not developed motivation in elementary school are able to pass, because they are closely supervised by their classroom teacher. With the decreased structure and supervision in middle school classrooms, the problems of these students intensify.* They float from one teacher to the next at school, slipping through the cracks of the educational system. Communication between home and school is usually less intensive, since students are expected to function autonomously. Students may become quite upset if parents go into the school to confer with their teachers. Youngsters who have not developed good study skills or the discipline to study regularly at home cannot cope with the increased emphasis on homework and studying in middle school. *Never having received recognition from adults for being outstanding students, many young adolescents are drawn toward the possibility of winning recognition from peers for being outstanding friends.*

Even children who are bright fall behind if they don't keep up with homework in the upper grades. Homework is often designed to teach new material, not just to reinforce material presented during the day, as in elementary school. Homework counts as part of the final semester grade, so it is not enough to do well on quizzes and tests. Students must turn in assignments or their grades suffer. Because of the increased homework load, deficiencies in organizational skills and ability to work independently become major handicaps at this age. Students who enter middle school with even a slight deficiency in reading or communication skills are at a serious disadvantage, since heavier loads of reading and writing are required in most academic classes. Unless they really dedicate themselves to studying and doing homework, they begin a downward academic slide.

"There's just too much homework, it's impossible to do it all," is a common refrain of middle school students. Parents of these students are often indignant about the tremendous homework load placed on their children. It is common for students to have five teachers, each one assigning thirty minutes of homework a night. Most parents agree this constitutes an unreasonable load for a sixth or seventh grade student. Children in this age group complain that the tremendous homework load is due to the fact that their many teachers don't communicate with one another and don't coordinate their homework schedules. On hearing this complaint, many parents become angry at the schools.

Middle school teachers do tend to assign hefty amounts of homework each night. However, most teachers provide class time for students to work on their assignments in school. Providing in-class time to begin homework enables teachers to give individual help and attention to those who need it and to answer questions while the rest of the class works independently. Those students who actually use the allotted time for doing homework usually can get their questions about the assignments answered, and can complete much of the homework.

Given the lack of social outlets for pre-teens, youngsters at this age are more interested in spending their "free" time in class socializing. This is especially true if they lack confidence and friends to begin with. Writing notes to one another, engraving their boyfriends' and girlfriends' names on their notebooks, and flirting take precedence over working on homework during class.

Even if they do start on homework in class, the girls aren't likely to get much done. Female adolescents are more concerned with form than substance. They use fancy markers and a large, swirling script when they write. Although they may misspell many words, they never fail to dot each "i" with a tiny heart or exaggerated loop. Engaging in the time-honored tradition of heart-drawing and note-writing takes up so much time, they can't make much progress on their assignments. The boys, of course, have a hard time getting very far on their assignments, since they may be too preoccupied with girls and sports to remember to take a pencil, paper, and textbook to class in the first place! Some students who don't get their work done in class simply take it home and hand it over to their parents to worry about. Or they don't take it home, and their parents worry even more!

Parents of these students try lectures of the "you're ruining your whole life" variety. But young adolescents ignore these lectures. They are concerned with peer relationships, as it seems to them that these are far more important for their future than academic success. Next parents try nagging. That doesn't work because by now, students have had many years to sharpen their skills at tuning out parents who nag.

Next, parents try to really get tough by grounding them from their friends. This is ineffective because at this age, children usually don't have many outside social activities (which is why they consider socializing at school so important). Also, young adolescents are sufficiently uncomfortable with peers that being separated from friends outside of the school environment is often a relief despite their protestations to the contrary. Further, most parents recognize the importance of allowing young adolescents to participate in those few social events which do occur. They find it difficult to remain firm over their youngster's pleas to have the punishment retracted until after the next skating party or slumber party.

For youngsters like Jake, academic difficulties are compounded by the social problems many children in his age group must confront. In truth, becoming comfortable with peers is an important developmental task of adolescence. Most pre-teens have a hard time remembering that success at school is as important as success in peer relationships.

It is imperative that parents support a young adolescents' attempts to solidify peer relationships while remaining firm about the need to do homework. Grounding a youngster from attending special activities with friends as punishment for not doing homework is unlikely to improve the situation and may make it worse. Most youngsters have very few planned events to attend since they have withdrawn from structured activities like scouts, piano lessons, and YMCA programs by this age. Prohibiting them from participating in the few social events that come up may give them cause to rebel.

Socially insecure youngsters may purposely not do homework so parents will ground them, thereby providing the excuse not to attend social activities. In therapy sessions, many confess they don't do their homework in hopes of being grounded! If they are required to stay home, they don't have to cope with so many social pressures. It is often easier for a youngster to say, "I can't go, I'm grounded," than to say, "I don't want to go. I'm interested in boys, but feel too shy to attend a party with them."

An easy way to determine if a child is avoiding homework and studying in hopes of being grounded is to look at what the child does when punished. If he seems just as happy being forced to stay at home, if grounding produces no improvement in behavior, the child's misbehavior may be a method for inducing parents to help him attain greater distance from peers.

Many pre-teenagers like Jake Smith want to be socially involved, but can't cope with the tremendous social pressures. Jake Smith's parents were right to worry about the questionable friends he was making. Jake really hadn't had much experience relating to children his age and couldn't productively handle so much peer contact. His desire to "be cool" and impress others to win friendships interfered with his ability to make good decisions about which friends and activities were constructive for him and which were destructive.

Many parents have a hard time determining when their child is ready to spend more time with peers and when the child needs less peer contact. Unfortunately, parents often make decisions about their children's ability to handle more peer contact based on their ability to handle school responsibilities. In reality, handling school responsibilities and handling social relationships are very different skills.

"If you do your homework this week, you can 'play' this weekend," parents may say. It is their way of saying, "work before pleasure." But learning to relate to peers is such an important developmental task of early adolescence, it may be considered important "work" for this age group. Teaching youngsters to balance school demands and social life is not easy. Parents need to develop other criteria besides academic achievement to determine their child's readiness for more peer contact. Grounding does not teach study skills! And few children who stay at home to serve out their sentences spend their time studying anyway.

Homework in High School:
The Case of Janet Brown

Janet was in a special school program for talented and gifted children in elementary school, was placed in several honors classes in middle school, and was immediately funneled into college preparatory classes in high school. A well-rounded, popular child, she seemed to excel in everything from sports to boyfriends to academics. Janet lived with her mother and two brothers during the week and visited her father on weekends. Her parents had divorced when she was nine.

Janet made the honor roll her freshman year of high school, made good grades in her sophomore classes even though swim team took up a lot of her time, but then suddenly fell apart her junior year. She withdrew from the swim team, dropped the friendships she had maintained since elementary school, changed her hairstyle, and stopped doing homework. By the end of junior year, her grades had fallen to the point where she was in danger of failing several classes.

"You're going to ruin your chances of getting into college," her mother warned Janet for the umpteenth time. Janet, who had provided a variety of lame excuses and vague promises that had left her parent feeling somewhat reassured, suddenly gave a reply that horrified Ms. Brown. "I've decided to get an apartment after high school and work for a year or two before continuing my education," she said.

Ms. Brown couldn't bear to see Janet make choices that would prevent her from fulfilling her childhood dreams (and Ms. Brown's dreams for her) on an adolescent whim. In the weeks that followed Ms. Brown did everything she could think of to get Janet to see the folly of her plan. She repeatedly bemoaned Janet's decision to give up swimming (which she had hoped would be Janet's ticket to a college scholarship), berated her new hair style (which she was sure must be as offensive to Janet's teachers as to herself), belittled her new-found friends (whom she felt were largely to blame for the problems). However, the endless "discussions" only impaired their ability to have a civil conversation on any subject. When Janet received two failing grades on her report card the first semester of her senior year, Ms. Brown reminded Janet that unless she shaped up she wouldn't even graduate with her class. Janet just shrugged and said that she didn't care!

Ms. Brown quickly learned what parents of teenagers everywhere have learned. Parents are unable to protect their children from the mistakes they seem determined to make. The Browns' many discussions weren't solving the problem, only jeopardizing their ability to communicate. If Janet was determined to fail, her mother could do nothing to stop her. It was at this point they sought professional counseling.

In my office, Janet was a very different person from the one her mother saw at home. I couldn't find the rebellious, hostile young woman her mother had described. Instead, I saw a scared little girl who was fearful of growing up and making her own way in the world. She talked with thinly disguised bravado about how anxious she was to be out on her own, free of parental demands and restrictions. Her behavior, however, said something very different: Janet was very clearly setting herself up to remain dependent on her mother for at least another year, if she failed school, and probably for several years to come, if she chose a low-paying job over a college career.

Janet was unquestionably avoiding the need to take responsibility for her life. Like many exceptionally able students, school had always been so easy for her, she hadn't had to discipline herself, make sacrifices, or establish goals. Never having had to exert herself to come out on top of any academic, social, or athletic heap, she was terrified of competition. In spite of an excellent record in elementary and middle school, she had little experience tackling difficult tasks and carrying them through to completion. Her study habits were poor. Jotting down a quick book report after having read the table of contents and a few pages of the book had enabled her to "ace" English assignments. Scanning a chapter in a textbook for five minutes before a test was all she needed to do well in other subjects. Overall, she had encountered few challenges in school and considered it "boring." In fact, she had been bored and understimulated through most of her school career. When a challenge did present itself, she was at a loss as to how to cope with the situation: When she lost an important race at a swim meet, her response was to quit the team.

In spite of her stellar SAT scores, the prospect of college terrified Janet, and she was sure she would flunk out. Janet realized she would have to push herself in college. She had often been accused of being lazy and feared that it was true. Setting a goal to get a minimum wage job reflected her true feelings about her capabilities: She didn't believe she could accomplish more.

Why was Janet so sure the skills that had enabled her to succeed from kindergarten to her sophomore year of high school wouldn't be sufficient for college? She had been told over and over by her parent and teachers that her haphazard attitude toward school "may work for you now, but you'll never make it in college." Of course, her parent and teachers may have been wrong. My guess was that Janet probably could succeed in college. Although her study habits were poor, her study skills were excellent. Her ability to do a maximum amount of work with a minimum expenditure of energy stemmed from her highly organized approach to learning tasks. She was an expert at selecting topic sentences, sorting important from incidental details, and synthesizing material. And, of course, she had intelligence and a strong command of reading, writing and math on her side. On the other hand, many exceptionally bright youngsters cannot succeed in college due to their poor study habits. In any case, Janet was convinced she would fail.

■ **Analysis.** Janet is typical of many students who believe they have fooled everyone into thinking they are capable. Despite good or excellent academic histories, they are sure they will fail the more rigorous tests ahead. Some give up and force failure rather than enter the next year in school where they believe they will be exposed.

"My teacher says if we don't write well, we'll never pass seventh grade," one youngster told me when I asked why he didn't seem to care about being retained in sixth grade. An eighth grader explained his reason for doing poorly. "In ninth grade they give exams on the whole year instead of tests on each chapter. It doesn't matter how well you do all year. If you fail the final exam, you fail. I'll never be able to remember things for a whole year. I don't want to go to high school." Although this youngster misunderstood high school grading policies, the logic is the same as that of older adolescents: Give up now to avoid failing later.

Those who have been told that they are not studying correctly and aren't really working for the grades they receive— but who have never been taught to approach their studies differently— may feel increasingly overwhelmed as the end of high school approaches, knowing they must soon make their way in college or "the real world." Being aware of their deficiencies, they live in fear of being overtaken by them. Indeed, students who have not learned to apply themselves, to manage time, to make a sustained effort, to tolerate failure, to create their own structure, to follow rules and limits, to function independently and responsibly may be overwhelmed by the exigencies of adult life.

A sudden deterioration in school performance may be a signal to parents that a child needs help learning to handle greater levels of responsibility. *Often it is the fear of failure combined with poor study skills, rather than poor academic skills alone, which account for serious problems in secondary school.*

Most high schools have alternative courses to serve students with deficient scholastic competencies. Remedial classes are offered in most schools. Vocational programs, emphasizing practical as opposed to strictly academic material, may help to reduce the pressure of heavy reading loads found in academic programs. Yet most classes still have homework. It doesn't matter whether a student is capable of doing the work. If he lacks self-confidence and has poor study skills, he may not be able to succeed.

It is not easy being a teenager, in any case, and other pressures compound homework problems. In some peer groups, it is considered unacceptable to study; even carrying books home may subject a youngster to ridicule. The urge to be accepted and well-liked remains an important goal of teenagers. Those whose friends do not support scholastic achievement have a hard time refusing to conform.

Family conflicts escalate during adolescence, as the process of emotional separation begins. Most parents and teenagers find themselves acting like couples who have decided to divorce. To confirm that their decision to part is really a good one, they begin taking special note of one another's flaws, arguing about petty issues, and finding it increasingly difficult to tolerate the closeness that will make it that much harder to leave. The societal expectation that growing up means moving out can be wrenching for parents and children alike.

Many adolescents hold jobs, are involved in extracurricular activities, and spend time with friends as well as attending school. They may have a hard time setting limits to ensure they give homework and studying the time and attention it deserves. Adolescents have increased freedom. Many drive cars, and parents may find their efforts to set limits fraught with difficulties. Adolescents need limits. They want limits. Yet they may thwart their parent's best efforts to set and enforce them. An adolescent's decision to comply is largely based on the quality of the parent-child relationship. The bottom line is that parents are helpless to control an adolescent. The adolescent must control himself.

**Homework Problems of the
Compulsive Studier:
The Case of Jerry Anderson**

Jerry's parents had a problem most of their friends envied: Jerry was a compulsive studier. Up until his sophomore year of high school, he came directly home from school, buried his nose in his books, and would have worked all evening long if left to his own devices. He was so terrified of making an error or handing in less than perfect work, he had a tantrum whenever he didn't understand some aspect of an assignment. Often, he would tear up his work and start from scratch. When a paper was to be completed in pen, Jerry refused to cross out an error and continue on, re-writing the entire paper instead. "The teacher said it's supposed to be neat," he insisted. Even when the teacher reassured Jerry (at the parents' request) that it was all right to make an error, Jerry was not reassured.

Study sessions in the Andersons' home had been fraught with con-stant bouts of tears, since Jerry began receiving homework in fourth grade. Jerry alternated between begging his parents for help and blaming them for not helping him correctly. Mr. and Mrs. Anderson didn't know how the problems began. Even in first grade Jerry cried in school when he missed a word on a spelling test. They weren't aware of having been overly demanding of him or of expecting perfection, although Mr. Anderson admitted to being somewhat of a perfectionist himself. "We were proud of his urge to excel. But he carried it to an extreme," he said of his son.

Jerry's perfectionism was basically confined to his studies, however. He could certainly tolerate his messy room, argued about having to take a bath in middle school years, and still didn't mind a smudge on his shirt. "It's just this crazy thing with homework," his mother said. "When his fifth grade teacher said the students could write a poem, a play, or a song for an extra-credit project, Jerry did all three!"

Jerry often stayed up so late working on (and worrying about) his school work, he was exhausted the next morning. This caused him to miss a lot of school, which resulted in more make-up work to be completed as homework.

"We tried to make him do homework in his room," said Mrs. Anderson, "but he came out into the living room every other minute asking for help. He either wanted to be sure he understood the assignment correctly, needed us to check his work, asked us to test him on his history vocabulary words, or required some other kind of assistance. Our evenings were a nightmare for years. If we made him go to bed before he finished studying, he got so upset he'd often be ill the next day and miss school. He would rather miss school altogether than go without an assignment. Once we made him go anyway, but the nurse called to say he was sick, so I had to bring him right back home."

In tenth grade, Jerry began having problems with his first period English class. His teacher gave him poor grades on his essays, and he couldn't seem to please her no matter how hard he tried. He began to develop headaches in the morning and would go late to school, missing her class. Some days he didn't go to school at all. He convinced his English teacher to give him a grade of incomplete, so he could finish the work the next semester. The next semester he continued to miss a lot of school, and his grades began to drop in all of his classes. He did not work on the missed English essays, and as the deadline for making up the incomplete grade approached, he became increasingly despondent. Soon he had missed so much school, he had fallen far behind in all of his classes.

"Perhaps it's my fault," said Mr. Anderson. "We kept telling him to relax and not work so hard. Probably we should have considered ourselves lucky to have such a conscientious child. But he was driving us crazy, not to mention what he was doing to himself. Now he's hardly doing anything at all."

■ **Analysis.** Students like Jerry have just as much of a problem with self-discipline as those who rarely sit down to do their homework. Whereas other children lack the self-discipline to begin doing work, Jerry lacked the self-discipline to stop. He had as little awareness of what constitutes a reasonable study session as his non-studying counterparts. He had as little concept of what constitutes acceptable homework papers, as the student who hands in work filled with messy scribbles and errors.

And like the parents of students in the previous case studies, Mr. and Mrs. Anderson were at a loss as to how to help their child. Despite their better judgement, they assumed much too much responsibility by explaining his assignments to him and checking his work. Rather than seeking other ways to spend time together, the focal point of their contact in the evening was homework. Although they repeatedly encouraged him to relax and tried to get him to work independently, they ended up supporting his compulsion to be "perfect." They never found a way to help him accept his limitations or explore what was causing him to drive himself so hard. Their hesitancy to discuss the problems with others kept them from finding solutions. When they tried to set limits, the intensity of Jerry's distress caused them to back down. Jerry never had the opportunity to learn that the world would not come to an end if he failed to complete all the extra credit, made some errors, or arrived at school unprepared. Although his parents repeatedly told him these things, he never experienced them himself. If his homework was incomplete or less than perfect, he simply missed school the next day. They even helped him by writing excuses, so he wouldn't get in trouble at school. The English teacher was never alerted to Jerry's problems. Taking the incomplete grade did not resolve the problem; it only served to postpone it and added to the pressure he was under.

Some students show fewer overt signs of distress than Jerry, yet display many of the same workaholic behaviors. Our culture has histori-cally revered and admired those who are obsessed by their jobs. Only in the last two decades have the physical and emotional tolls of such attitudes been exposed. Studies of adults who overindulge in work indicate what Jerry's parents knew all along: Workaholics don't accomplish much more than their more relaxed peers. Their tendency to overindulge in work causes them to become ill a lot, resulting in periods of little accomplishment. Their inability to focus on what is important and to prioritize their work frequently leads them to mismanage their time. Their belief that they must be perfect leaves them little joy from their endeavors.

Learning to cope with one's limitations is important. Even more important is learning to value oneself despite imperfections. Students who do not learn to do this experience exaggerated fears of failing. Students who put too much pressure on themselves and fail to attend to their physical and emotional health may collapse under their self-imposed pressure.

Chapter 4

Towards
Better
Communication

When parents and children talk about homework, the same conversations tend to repeat themselves.

"I feel like a broken record," parent after parent complains.

"I talk until I'm blue in the face," say others.

"I think we've reached an understanding, then the same problem comes up again," some parents complain.

"I get so frustrated I could scream," many confess.

"I get so frustrated, I do scream," still others admit.

There are two ways to communicate with a child about homework — with words and with actions. What parents do is much more important than what parents say, when it comes to ensuring that children are responsible about doing their homework. Nevertheless, how parents talk to their youngsters makes a difference in children's willingness to cooperate. Even though verbal discussions do not provide a total solution, parents need to be sure that their conversations are working for them and not, as is so often the case, against them.

There are many books on the market and courses sponsored through PTAs and other organizations that teach communication skills to improve parent-child relationships. Yet even parents who have read these books and taken such courses have a hard time applying the techniques to nightly discussions about homework. This may be due, in part, to the fact that homework is such a highly charged issue in so many homes. It may also be because homework is really a very complex issue.

To combat the "broken record syndrome" and break the cycle of communication that goes nowhere, it is necessary to first understand the dynamics of power struggles. When parents sound like broken records, it is usually because they are caught up in a power struggle with their youngster.

Power Struggles

When a child handles his displeasure over homework by arguing, it is called a verbal or overt power struggle. When a child uses passive-resistance to express his feelings, it is called a non-verbal or covert power struggle. The child may lose his books, forget his assignments at school, purposely race through his homework or do poor work.

Covert power struggles over homework take many forms. Some youngsters comply when parents threaten or punish to get them to study. However, the youngsters proceed to argue about other issues later in the evening or act out their anger by struggling with teachers or misbehaving at school the next day. It is not always clear to parents that many other problems with their child actually stem from conflicts over homework.

Parents struggle to get their children to do homework because they understand that their duty is to ensure that children handle this responsibility. Such struggles degenerate into contests of wills. Parents become caught up in power struggles when they feel threatened or intimidated. When this happens, parents are likely to be reacting to pressure from teachers, from their children, or from themselves.

Power struggles may also develop between parents and teachers. Although this chapter focuses on eliminating power struggles between parents and children by improving parent/child communication, the same skills may be applied to reducing teacher/parent conflicts. Parents may teach their youngsters to use these communication skills to improve relationships with their teachers.

The Fight or Flight Response

The human response to situations which cause them to feel threatened or attacked is so uniform, it has been dubbed the "fight or flight" response. Psychologists hypothesize that the urge to fight or flee to cope with perceived threats is innate and may have had evolutionary value: When our cave man ancestors were faced with a threat from their environment such as that posed by a menacing saber-toothed tiger, a surge of adrenalin enhanced their ability to fight or flee to defend themselves.

The threats people face today are more often emotional than physical, but the responses are the same as the cave man's: When they feel threatened by another's words or actions, adrenalin is released into the bloodstream, preparing them to fight or flee. The result is that people either assume a defensive posture and argue (fight) or seek to escape the threat by avoiding it altogether (flight). If it is not possible to do either, the continuing surges of adrenalin may weaken the immune system and erode physical health.

Criticism and Blame

Being criticized causes children to feel threatened, thereby increasing the likelihood they will defend themselves by fighting (engaging in power struggles) or fleeing (avoiding homework or the parent altogether). Sometimes it is hard for parents to understand that criticism is threatening to children and does more harm than good, since "constructive criticism" is regarded as a valuable teaching tool. Indeed, constructive criticism is useful when it involves analyzing a student's work and giving feedback and advice. If a student who is having trouble understanding *The Merchant of Venice* asks for assistance, he may benefit from parental comments such as, "It may help you to read each section a few times, underline parts you still don't understand, and discuss them. It may also help if you turn your radio off when you read, so you can give the book your full attention."

Criticism which makes children feel badly about themselves is destructive since it threatens their self-esteem, thereby activating their "fight or flight" response. If a parent responds to the question about *The Merchant of Venice* by saying, "You're always complaining about something," or "You just want me to do your thinking for you. Figure it out yourself," children experience a blow to their egos. Some argue to try to defend themselves. "But even my teacher says Shakespeare's hard," they may say, or "Even John can't understand parts of it, and he's the smartest kid in the class." Others will engage in covert power struggles by losing their books or lashing out about another issue later. Still others "flee" the situation by retreating to their rooms and avoiding further conversations with the parent who has caused them to feel badly about themselves. They may avoid *The Merchant of Venice*, because it serves as a painful reminder of the conversation. The book itself may now seem threatening. The student may attribute his difficulties understanding the story to the deficiencies of his own character noted by the parent. He may interpret his feelings of frustration as signs that he is lazy or bad.

Parental responses that involve blame cause children to fight or flee, resulting in power struggles, too. Blame is much like criticism in that it also involves finding fault. In blaming a child, parents also imply or state that the child has caused his own problems. "If you spent more time reading and less time talking on the phone to your friends, you might not find Shakespeare so hard," is an example of a blaming response. Although these may be true statements that enable parents to vent some of their own frustrations, they rarely serve to motivate a child. It is a rare child who, after being blamed in this way, says, "Gee, you're right! I guess I'll give up talking on the phone until I've finished the book and passed the test." Instead, children who feel they are being blamed try to defend themselves and may argue the point — if they are still speaking to their parents at all.

Parents who are out of touch with their own feelings may not realize how critical or blaming they sound when asking questions or making comments about homework. They are shocked to discover that their innocent comments could be threatening. Thousands of therapists have spent millions of therapy hours trying to increase parents' awareness of how they come across to their children.

As one adolescent said to his mother, "When I asked if I could go to Jane's house and you asked me if I had any homework, it seemed like you were telling me I'm so irresponsible that you need to check up on me." In fact, after the adolescent made this statement, the parent immediately cited several examples of times the youngster had acted irresponsibly regarding homework. The parent's comment served to confirm the child's suspicions that the "innocent question" really did contain an element of criticism.

Some children are more sensitive than others and feel criticized and blamed during conversations about homework, even though the parent does not mean to be critical or judgmental. The most important criteria for judging whether a parent's statement is critical or blaming can't be determined by objective analysis. The criteria is the way the statement makes the child feel. There are times when parents do not mean to be critical, are not feeling critical, yet the child is upset by a parent's comment anyway. Feelings are not necessarily rational. They just are. There are no "shoulds" or "oughts" for feelings (although of course there are many "shoulds" and "oughts" that guide behavior). Since every child is unique, responses that some children perceive as critical may be viewed as innocuous by others, regardless of the parent's intention.

An example may be helpful to illustrate this point. While meeting with a father and his two sons for a counseling session to discuss the boys' school problems, the subject of homework came up. "And they're both so lazy!" the father said. "When I was growing up, we did our work or there was hell to pay." The older child grimaced slightly, so I asked how he felt about what his father had just said. "He's always saying things like that, putting me down and criticizing me. He never notices when I do anything right." Thus, it was obvious that the first boy experienced his father's remark as critical. I asked the younger child how he felt about his father's comment, to which the child replied, "Oh, that's just Dad. He worries a lot about us."

The School of Hard Knocks

There are parents who believe children must learn to accept criticism and think it is wrong to allow children to communicate displeasure about having to do homework or their frustrations with the work itself. "Sure it bothers me to see my child hurt or upset," they say, "but that's life. It's not a bed of roses." In hopes of strengthening children's characters, these parents may react critically to expressions of displeasure over assigned tasks or chores. "When the going gets tough, the tough get going...only the losers waste their time weeping and wailing," they say. Such parents may also fear that if they let their children know how much they love them, the children may grow up to be weak; if they provide praise for accomplishments, they will become conceited; if they empathize with their problems, they will wallow in self-pity.

Parents who perceive the world as a dangerous place may feel a need to prepare their youngsters by providing a home environment devoid of warmth or tenderness. "What was good enough for me is good enough for my child," some say, recalling how little emotional support they received from their own parents. "I grew up in the school of hard knocks, and I don't regret it," several parents have told me. "It got me where I am today." Yet, I have often wondered if the graduates of that particularly brutal school might not have gotten even further in life had they had a bit more support early on.

In fact, people who remember their childhood homes as having been warm, supportive places where they felt accepted are happier and better adjusted as adults. Too often, hard times and hard knocks beat children down rather than strengthening them. They expend so much energy struggling to survive, cope and overcome, they have fewer resources to dedicate to growing and thriving.

In any case, some approaches may work well with some children but fail abysmally with others. Parents who have tried raising their children in "the school of hard knocks" and are still having problems getting them to do homework responsibly would be well-advised to try a different approach. Permitting a bit of weeping, wailing, and belly-aching before starting study sessions may well produce a more cooperative, motivated child. If not, the hang-tough approach can always be reinstated after a softer approach has been given a fair (one month) try.

Eliminating Power Struggles

To eliminate power struggles over homework, parents must find ways to remove the sting of criticism from their communications. To do this, they must:

1 Avoid being critical or casting blame during conversations.

2 Watch for signs that the child is feeling criticized or blamed, and strive to clear up misunderstandings.

3 Strive to make amends after having responded in a critical or blaming way.

In the example of the teenager who felt criticized whenever his mother asked if he had homework, the mother was able to tell her youngster that every time she posed such a question she was not commenting on his ability to behave responsibly. "I just feel it is my duty to stay informed about your studies. Even if you were 100 percent conscientious about doing homework, I'd still want to ask you about it from time to time just so I'd know what is happening in your life." Since the mother was apt to become critical when she was having a hard time dealing with her own frustrations and did not believe criticizing her son to be a helpful response, she agreed to apologize if she responded critically. They worked out an agreement wherein the child would tell his mother whenever he felt criticized and she would then tell him whether he was correct or not.

Writing It Out

To improve communication it is important to determine the kinds of comments a particular child experiences as critical or blaming. I recommend parents sit down with their children and say something like, "When we talk about your homework, I may make statements that make you feel as though I am criticizing or blaming you. I would like us to be able to talk more openly with one another. To improve our communication I realize I must try not to say things that hurt your feelings or make you feel criticized. I'd like you to take a moment to write down some things I've said in the past on the subject of homework that have upset you."

Although this exercise is useful for many parents, it certainly is not appropriate for everyone. Receiving constructive criticism from children can be threatening to parents and hard for many to accept. Some parents believe it is inappropriate for children to comment on parental behavior under any circumstances. Deciding whether or not to ask for feedback is difficult. Parents need to determine whether they can receive the criticism without becoming unduly upset, using what they learn to improve communication in the future.

Most children are hesitant to provide this kind of feedback. In doing so, they are taking an obvious risk, for they are saying, "Here is a list of things that hurt me." Anyone who provides another human being with a list of things that can hurt him is placing himself in an extremely vulnerable position. Unless parents are careful in subsequent discussions, they may further impair their relationship with their youngster.

Once parents have received their children's lists they can sort the information into four categories.

1 The first category consists of items which the parent readily recognizes as containing elements of blame or criticism. Often parents are sure they never said some of the things their children report having heard. Whether parents remember the comments or not, it is helpful if they can set a new tone for future communication by apologizing and saying, "I'm sorry I said that to you. That must have hurt your feelings," or "I don't remember having said that, and I am very sorry that is what you heard. That must have hurt a lot." Then, I recommend parents express an intention to avoid making similar statements in the future by saying, "I'm going to try not to say these things to you in the future, but if I am in a bad mood I might forget. If I do repeat them, would you help me out by reminding me? You can just say, 'Mom, remember that it upsets me when you say that.'"

Note that parents should avoid making blanket promises to refrain from making critical or blaming comments in the future. Old habits take a while to change.

2 The second category of items appearing on children's lists are those which the parent does not view as critical or blaming. Ask your child about these items to discover exactly what caused him to feel upset. One child wrote, "When you tell me to go do my homework," on his list. When the parent asked why that comment made the child feel upset, he responded, "Because you sound mad when you say it." After talking about other ways the parent could communicate the same message without sounding critical, they agreed that if the parent smiled and said, "It's time to do your homework" rather than frowning and saying, "Go do it," the child would not feel hurt. When parents order and command their children to do things, children often feel criticized.

3 The third category of items consists of those the parent is unable to change. One teenaged girl felt "mad" when she asked the parent for help and the parent's explanations were unclear. The daughter felt criticized when the parent gave up, as though the mother was saying, "You're not smart enough to learn this." After discussing a variety of options, no conclusion was reached. They agreed to continue searching for solutions.

4 The fourth category includes items which the parent is unwilling to change. "It makes me feel hurt when you tell me to turn off the radio when I'm doing my homework," one child wrote. The child said he felt criticized because the parent didn't enforce the same rule for an older sibling.

The parent had set a different rule for the younger child who was very distractible. His mother explained this to the child, but it didn't help. Any reminders of his problem caused him to feel criticized. "It sounds like your mother wants to keep this rule. Is there anything she can do to help you feel better about it?" I asked. The child's suggestions were not acceptable to the parent, so it appeared as though this child would just have to cope as best he could.

Then I said to the mother, "You know, most parents believe they should feel the same about all of their children, but most actually like some things better about one child and some things better about another one. Are there any things you especially like about this child?" The mother responded by saying, "Well, because he's my youngest, I've always felt a special sort of closeness between us. He tells great jokes, and he's very affectionate. My older son doesn't like me to hug him anymore, but my younger one still lets me hug him." The youngster was obviously delighted by his mother's response. They agreed that whenever his mother told him to turn off the radio, she would give him a hug to help him remember some of the things she found special about him.

Thinking It Out

Parents who decide not to ask their children for feedback can simply do a bit of soul searching in an effort to identify critical or blaming statements they have made in the past when discussing homework. Those parents who are having a hard time identifying their contribution to the power struggle should try to determine their feelings and tone of voice used during problematic conversations. If a parent is feeling angry or sounds gruff, children are likely to perceive criticism, regardless of the actual words spoken.

In addition, parents should pause when they sense communication breaking down and ask their child what is upsetting him. Again, parents need to be careful how they handle subsequent information. Too often when parents hear the responses, they begin defending themselves, saying something like, "All I said was, 'why don't you ask your teacher when you don't understand an assignment?'" *Yet, the problem is not with what a parent says. The problem is with what a child feels.* When parents defend themselves, the power struggle continues. It is more helpful for parents to say, "I'm sorry if I sounded like I was blaming you. What I meant is that it would help if you could find the courage to ask your teacher when you don't understand something. I wish I could give you that courage and make you less afraid of her."

Three Ways of Discussing Homework

To improve communication about homework and combat the "broken record syndrome," it helps to understand the three main categories of communication:

1 Cognitive — the level of knowledge

2 Emotional — the level of feelings

3 Behavioral — the level of actions

When a child talks about homework, he speaks either about his cognitive understanding (what he knows or does not know), about his emotions (what he feels or does not feel), or of his actions (what he is or is not doing). When a child says, "I know I should do my homework," he is speaking on the cognitive level because he is communicating about what he knows, thinks, or logically understands. When a child says, "But I hate doing homework," he is speaking at the emotional level and is communicating about his feelings. When he says, "I'm not doing my homework," he is talking about actions and is communicating at the behavioral level.

To respond productively, parents need to be able to correctly categorize the child's communication and respond to that level, before making a statement of their own. Otherwise, communications become confusing and frustrating, and conversations are likely to escalate into arguments or deteriorate into power struggles as in the following example.

Child: I wish I didn't have any homework. (expressing feelings)
Parent: Go do it now. (discussing actions)
Child: But— (about to express feelings)
Parent: If you don't do it, you'll make bad grades! (providing information at the cognitive level)

This brief conversation will probably leave the child feeling frustrated, and perhaps a bit angry and misunderstood. The child was talking on the emotional level — he was describing his feelings. The parent did not respond to what the child said and switched the subject twice, first to discuss actions, next to appeal to the child's cognitive understanding.

Taking a moment to respond at the same level (in this case, to the child's feelings) can change the tone of the conversation, even though the parent communicates the same "action" message later on.

Child: I wish I didn't have any homework.

Parent: I know, it's not much fun to have more school work to do after the school day is over. You do need to get started on it, however.

The child may still not want to do homework, but at least he knows he has been heard and understood. He need not go to greater lengths to communicate his dissatisfaction. He won't feel personally criticized by the parent's statement, which often would have set the stage for a power struggle.

Before parents can gear their responses to make sure they are speaking on the same level as the child, they must have an in-depth understanding of each kind of communication.

Communicating about Emotions

When communicating at the emotional level, children strive to share their reaction to experiences. When parents respond to a child who is communicating at the emotional level, they speak and respond like a friend or therapist.

Most parents have a hard time responding adequately when their child is communicating on an emotional level. In fact, many parents have difficulty even grasping that emotions are involved in homework. "If he knows why he needs to do his homework, why doesn't he just do it?" countless parents ask.

Yet it is readily apparent that all of us, at one time or another, don't do what we know we really should do because often we operate on an emotional level. We know we should mow the lawn this weekend, but still we put it off. We know we should cook at home instead of running to a restaurant for a take-out meal, but still we opt for fast-food. We know we shouldn't speed, but most of us have driven faster than the law permits at one time or another. The reason is simple. We don't do what we're supposed to do because we don't feel like it. Perhaps we are feeling too bored, tired, lazy, inadequate, rebellious, or pressured. Perhaps we'd prefer to do something else instead. Perhaps we can't quite define the feeling: We only know we don't want to do something we know we should do. None of this is said to excuse misbehavior, but merely to point out that all of us misbehave at times. Occasionally we misbehave because we don't know what we are supposed to do, but most often it is because our feelings are interfering. An important part of growing up and maturing is learning how to express feelings productively so they do not dominate our behavior.

As I counsel parents of problem studiers, most are mystified by their children's unwillingness to dedicate themselves to homework. "I just don't know what the problem is," they say. Whenever I point out that most children do not enjoy homework, these parents commonly reply, "But he has to do it!" If I attempt to clarify the conversation by saying, "Yes, he has to do homework, but like most children he probably wishes he didn't have to," many parents become openly hostile. "But he has got to do it!" they proclaim, as if I am in disagreement on this point. Other parents are more soft spoken, but their attitude suddenly changes. The moment I try to talk about feelings and say, "Most children don't enjoy homework," they see me as a questionable character who might corrupt their child. I receive many lectures from parents about the importance of doing homework — as if I'm not already convinced!

Feelings and Actions

Why would my simple statement provoke such a reaction? These parents are confusing *feelings* with *actions*. When I say children don't *like* homework, they assume I am saying children need not *do* homework. As communication disintegrates, they begin speaking on the level with which they are most comfortable, the cognitive level, and lecture about the importance of homework.

The tendency to confuse feelings, actions, and cognitions which occurs in my office, happens at home as well. If a child says, "I wish the teachers didn't assign so much homework," the parents may react by becoming angry and delivering lectures about the importance of studying. They are unable to tolerate their children's statements about disliking homework, since to them it is the same as tolerating their children not doing homework.

Parents who are having a hard time grasping the difference between feelings and actions often say, "But if he doesn't like homework or want to study, he won't do the work." Of course, there are many things children don't want to do that they must do anyway, such as take medicine, wear a raincoat, or observe a curfew. Helping children mature emotionally involves teaching them to handle feelings, so the feelings don't interfere with responsible behavior. Therefore, it is imperative that parents seek ways to communicate, "It's fine not to like homework; still, you must do it."

The following scene is being played out in many homes night after night.

Parent: Time to do your homework. You have a spelling test tomorrow.

Child: Aw, shucks. I hate having to write out all those words five times each. It's a waste of time. (Note that the child is expressing feelings.)

Parent:	If you don't write them out like you're supposed to, you're going to fail your test tomorrow. (The parent has responded by talking about actions.) You'll never get anywhere in life if you don't apply yourself! (The lecture begins.)
Child:	But writing out all those words takes so long. Anyway, I already know how to spell them all. (The child is still expressing feelings, a bit more strongly now, trying to get the parent to understand. He is shifting to the cognitive level by telling "what he knows," but he's doing a poor job of it.)
Parent:	Get busy now! In the time you spend arguing about it, you could have had half the words done! (But the child wasn't arguing about doing the work, at least not at first. He was expressing his feelings.) All you want to do is play. Don't you care if you fail your test tomorrow? (Another lecture begins. Now who is wasting time?)
Child:	O.K., but can I stay up late and watch a movie? (Where in the world did this question come from? Is the child angry about being lectured to, and retaliating by provoking the parent? Or stalling a bit longer? Or giving the parent yet another chance to demonstrate sympathy by granting a special privilege?)

The Importance of Communicating about Feelings

"He still has to do homework! Talking about feelings won't make the work go away," parents point out.

While it's true that talking won't make the work go away and hearing children express negative feelings can be uncomfortable for parents, there are a number of reasons why it is important that parents listen.

★ Talking provides a safety valve which enables children to discharge the tension they experience when they are upset about having to do chores they find unpleasant. There is a saying among therapists that "feelings that don't get talked out get acted out." *Children who are forbidden to verbalize their feelings or are reprimanded for discussing their dislike of homework often engage in covert power struggles to get their feelings out or their message across.* Often this takes the form of not doing the work.

★ Children are more cooperative about doing their work if an adult listens to and respects their feelings. There is a kind of validation that takes place when a parent accepts children's feelings which serves to deepen and strengthen the parent-child relationship. They feel less alone, and difficult chores often feel more manageable.

★ All feelings (including "negative" ones like anger and sadness) are inherently good in that they provide important information about what is happening inside us. To say feelings are "bad" is like saying the gas gauge on a car is bad for signaling that the car is out of gas. While most children don't like homework, those who despise it with a passion may have a learning problem, may be receiving assignments which are too lengthy or too difficult, or have another problem which needs to be resolved. Unless parents listen and even encourage children to say more, they won't be able to help them identify such problems.

Constructive Responses at the Emotional Level

The first step to responding on the emotional level, then, is eliminating destructive responses that cause the child to feel criticized or blamed. The second step is to employ constructive responses which result in productive discussions. *Constructive responses are those which let the child know he has been heard and which communicate warmth, empathy, and positive regard for the child's feelings.*

There are two main categories of constructive responses:

1 Responses that provide acknowledgement

2 Responses that provide support

Acknowledgement

The typical reaction to not being heard or understood is to repeat oneself. Parents who do not let their child know they have been heard often complain that the youngster "carries on about the same old thing," when, in fact, the child does not believe he has been heard. When this happens, children sound like broken records.

Most parents find it easiest to provide acknowledgement. However, there is a tendency for women to communicate acknowledgement more readily than men, so men in particular may need to exert extra effort to ensure they are actually verbalizing a response. (Often men "think" their responses rather than speaking them.)

There are three ways to provide acknowledgement:

■ **"Uh-huh."** The simplest way to acknowledge a child's response is to say "I understand," "I know," "I guess that's probably true," "Uh-huh," "Oh?" or to nod while making direct eye contact. (Parents who continue reading the newspaper while giving a verbal response will not convince children they have actually heard them.)

The biggest complaint among adolescents is, "My parents never listen to me." While sometimes what teenagers are really seeking is agreement from parents, often they aren't receiving acknowledgement for having spoken and are longing simply to know they've been heard.

Parents are sometimes reluctant to provide acknowledgement for fear the child will mistake their response as agreement, and so they say nothing at all. It is true that children who are not accustomed to being acknowledged by their parents may be confused at first as to what the parent means. If a child says "I'm too tired to study" and the parent nods, it is possible that some children will interpret the nod to mean it is all right for them to pass up studying that evening.

This confusion is especially common among children who have not been taught to differentiate feelings and actions. To them, "feeling" something means the same as "doing" it. Parents can clear up any resulting confusion by saying, "I understand that you feel too tired to do homework, but you still must study."

■ **Restatement.** Another way to provide acknowledgement is to restate what the child has just said by simply parroting back or summarizing the content of the statement. While parents often feel awkward and uncomfortable responding in this way ("You mean, I just say the very same thing over again? That seems foolish!"), they typically find it is not only quite difficult to do but has some unexpected results.

Repeating what was said is difficult because even though most of us think we are good listeners, when we attempt to repeat or summarize, we discover we either did not hear correctly or missed the speaker's point altogether. This is due to not paying close enough attention, "assuming" what the speaker really meant since it was similar to things they said before, or indulging our tendency to immediately interpret the content. In interpreting, we add our own ideas, thereby distorting the information.

When parents do succeed at accurately restating their child's main point, they are often surprised to find that this type of response also encourages the child to say more. *Restatement opens lines of communication rather than cutting them off;* the results can be quite dramatic. In my office, one father and son role-played a conversation they had at home.

Father: Time to do homework.
Son: Gee, can I do it later? I'm really tired now.

Father:	Do you want to take a nap?
Son:	No. Can I go out and play?
Father:	Then you're not tired! You're just trying to manipulate your way out of your responsibilities again!

Both father and son ended up feeling upset. When the father used restatement, the conversation ended quite differently.

Father:	Time to do homework.
Son:	Gee, can I do it later? I'm really tired now.
Father:	You want to do it later because you're tired.
Son:	Yeah. P.E. was canceled because our teacher was sick today, and I had a piano lesson after school, so I didn't get to play at all. I want to ride my bike for a while, first.

In the first example, the father heard "sleepy" although the child actually said "tired." Or perhaps the father interpreted "tired" from his own perspective, which to him meant a need for sleep. The father overlooked the fact that for his son, as for most children, sitting is more tiring than engaging in physical activities. Note that the father may still decide his son needs to do homework rather than play. But if he can say, "I understand how tired you are, but still you must start your study period," the child won't need to expend additional time or energy proving how tired he is. There is less likelihood of a power struggle developing than if the father ends the conversation by implying his son was lying.

■ **Clarification.** The third way to provide acknowledgement is using clarification. In clarification the parent attempts to better understand what the child has said. Most of us do not use this response nearly enough. Instead we jump to conclusions, assume what is meant, and end up actually creating conflict rather than eliminating it. (Therapists have their own definition of the word "assume": "to make an ass of u and me.")

Clarification responses begin with the words, "You mean that," followed by a summary of what the parent thinks the child said. Like restatement, it encourages the speaker to say more, thus opening communication rather than cutting it off.

Usually parents need to clarify each statement three to four times to fully understand the child's communication. They are to continue clarifying until the child nods or says, "Yes, that's right." Here is an example of a mother using a clarifying response.

Daughter:	I don't see why we need to learn algebra. It's stupid.
Mother:	You mean that you don't want to study for your test tomorrow?

Daughter: It's just that algebra seems like a waste of time.

Mother: You mean that you have other things you'd rather be doing.

Daughter: I don't like algebra because it has nothing to do with real life.

Mother: You mean that if it seemed more relevant, you wouldn't mind learning it.

Daughter: Well, I'm not sure I'd like it even then, but I wouldn't mind spending so much time studying it.

Mother: You mean that you don't think you'd ever like algebra, but you'd be more willing to study if you thought learning algebra served some purpose.

Daughter: Yes.

Had this mother not used clarifying responses to better understand her daughter, she would have assumed that her daughter was just being lazy. Had the mother verbalized her thoughts, a power struggle would most likely have ensued. After having clarified what the daughter really meant, the mother may then explain the benefits of knowing algebra in everyday life or suggest she ask her teacher to explain them.

When parents clarify children's communications in an attempt to better understand them, they also help children become clearer about their own thoughts and feelings. This helps them pinpoint and define problems with which they may need help. Thus, as parents help children clarify their meanings, they are also helping them take the first step toward solving the problems.

Providing Support

The two kinds of constructive responses which provide emotional support are empathetic responses and sympathetic responses.

■ Empathy. When a parent empathizes with a child, he tries to understand the totality of his child's experience to the point that he can see the world through the child's eyes. Such profound understanding often causes children to feel a special closeness to their parent. Feelings of aloneness disappear; they feel emotionally supported long after the conversation has ended. Empathy strengthens children, enabling them to confront difficulties on their own.

When parents respond empathetically, they not only open lines of communication to their youngster, they also help the child become more aware of his own feelings. Such awareness is a necessary first step to dealing with troublesome emotions.

Empathetic responses begin with the words, "you're feelings," followed by an adjective such as tired, worried, sad, hurt, frustrated, irritated, proud, happy, hopeful, disgusted, anxious, fearful, delighted, jealous, ill, relieved, encouraged. The parent's tone of voice must reflect the youngster's feeling, showing him that the parent truly understands. A parent who says, "You're feeling sad," while smiling broadly will not sound as though he understands anything at all.

To respond empathetically, parents can not sound judgmental or critical. Instead, their tone must be warm and accepting. They must communicate that it is truly all right to have those feelings.

If a parent says, "You're feeling jealous because your sister doesn't have homework," the tone may communicate that this is a bad way to feel. The parent's response is critical, not empathetic. On the other hand, the parent's tone may communicate that the child's feeling is natural and normal. Parents who have responded critically to their children in the past may need to change their tone and clarify their meaning, saying, "You're feeling jealous of your sister, and that is certainly understandable." Otherwise, children may color the parent's comments with the shades of meaning they have gleaned from previous conversations, and react accordingly.

Empathetic responses may sound like clarifying responses. The difference between the two is subtle. In clarification, parents respond to the content or general meaning of the child's communication to determine what was said. In empathizing, parents focus on restating the child's *feelings* rather than the overall content.

Parents usually feel awkward responding in new and different ways. They often sound like parrots rather than understanding adults, until they become accustomed to responding empathetically. It is important for parents to continue trying to respond in this new way, since empathy is a potent response for improving parent-child relationships and helping children. In the following dialogue, the parent's words may sound hollow and artificial or may display concern, depending on the tone of voice.

Son: I hate science.
Mother: You really dislike it.
Son: Yeah. My science partner likes to play around, and he messes up the experiments.
Mother: That sounds like it must be frustrating.
Son: Yes. Then I get bad grades on the lab reports, even though it's not my fault.
Mother: That doesn't seem fair.
Son: Yes. I wish I had a different lab partner.

A closer look at the above dialogue shows that the son was helped to more clearly identify his feelings: He changed from saying "I hate science" to expressing dissatisfaction with his lab partner. Perhaps he knew at the beginning of the conversation that it was his lab partner's actions, rather than science in general, that he disliked. It is hard to know whether he was aware of his feelings at the outset or not. Too often children conclude, "I hate English" when what they really dislike is grammar, or they decide, "I hate math" when what they really dislike is their teacher's method of grading. Parents are fulfilling an important responsibility in helping children identify their true feelings.

It is equally important to respond empathetically when children express happy feelings. "I only have a couple of math problems to do tonight!" says Johnny, smiling and beaming. "I finished the rest in school." Often parents miss the opportunity to praise the child or to respond empathetically by saying, "How wonderful that must feel." It is common for parents to say instead, "Then go finish the rest of your work. You need to clean your room tonight, too." The message to the child is, "I am not interested unless there is a problem." Other children conclude, "It doesn't matter what I do; I can't ever please my parents."

Perhaps the most important effect of empathetic responses is that they provide emotional support. The notion that "my parent understands how I feel" strengthens children and can lighten their load to the point that they are able to suddenly manage tasks and handle situations that felt over-whelming prior to discussing them *even though the parent doesn't try to actually solve the child's problem.* Counselors and therapists are taught how to respond empathetically during their training, and even seasoned therapists are sometimes surprised at clients' abilities to cope with very difficult situations and rectify their own problems, once they receive an empathetic response.

■ **Sympathy.** How to encourage a child who is feeling overwhelmed by the demands of school and homework? Providing sympathy occurs so natu-rally in communication with adults and even with other people's children, I have never understood the tendency for many parents to refrain from expressing sympathy to their own family members. Sympathy is very effective in soothing children when they are upset or distressed. Examples of sympathetic responses include, "Gee, that's too bad," "I'm sorry to hear that," "That must be hard on you," "What a terrible thing to have happen," "I wish there were something I could do or say to help you feel better," "I hope it gets better for you." I've never yet met anyone who was damaged by a sympathetic word. Sympathy helps fortify a child emotionally, providing additional strength for facing trying situations.

Children who are consistently nurtured and comforted by parental expressions of sympathy learn to nurture and comfort themselves. Like empathetic responses, sympathy lets the child know he is entitled to his feelings by the tone of voice used as well as by the words. Parents who speak with sarcasm or irritation do not sound sympathetic. The capacity for sympathetic responses to reduce power struggles is so great that I have presented several examples below, along with responses in which parents criticize or blame. Critical responses escalate power struggles; sympathetic responses diffuse them.

Child: I can't believe our term papers are due right after Christmas! That means I'll have to spend the vacation studying!

Parent 1:   (Sympathizing) That really is a shame.

Parent 2:   (Blaming) It's your own fault! You should have started on it long ago.

Child: I have to take a written test in gym. Gym is supposed to be for playing, not for taking tests.

Parent 1:   (Sympathizing) That's too bad. It kind of takes the fun out of P.E., doesn't it?

Parent 2:   (Criticizing) You think everything's supposed to be fun. You never want to work at anything.

Proceeding with Care

There are several dangers in empathizing or sympathizing with a child's feelings about homework (or anything else, for that matter). Although I am firmly convinced of the merits of doing so, there are some side effects which can be distressing to parents. Consider them carefully before you attempt to change the way you discuss homework with your child.

★ *Children who have been criticized for expressing their feelings suppress much anger, frustration, and sadness over many different issues through the years.* When a parent begins to tolerate expressions of feelings for the first time, it is like taking the proverbial finger out of the dike: Accumulated feelings come bursting forth. This can be unnerving to parents. Although this stage is a temporary one for the child, parents sometimes hear things that cause them to feel upset for a long time. Jane's mother serves as an example.

"Jane started talking about not wanting to prepare her oral report for social studies. Instead of cutting her off like I usually do, I let her talk. Then she told me why she refuses to speak in front of the class. It turns out she had a third grade teacher who really humiliated her when she gave a book report, going so far as to make fun of Jane and encouraging the other children to join in. If only I had known! I feel terrible that I never gave her opportunities to talk about this before. She took failing grades on every oral report since then, rather than risk getting up in front of the class. And I've been humiliating her, too, calling her crazy for taking F's instead of giving the reports she spends so much time preparing.

★ *Children who have not been allowed to express angry feelings in the past may not know how to do so appropriately.* Often they use the same language they use when talking to friends, since the only time they have been permitted to verbalize anger was in their friends' presence. In some peer groups it may be acceptable to say, "I hate that damned French teacher," while many parents find such language unacceptable for use at home. Parents must respond to the feelings expressed, while teaching their children appropriate language. To simply scold is to risk communicating, "It is wrong to talk about feeling angry." Too many children end up in counseling sessions to learn how to express their anger productively.

★ *Parents may find themselves switching loyalties.* When parents allow children to express their dislike of homework and help them express their worries and concerns about it, parents may find themselves switching loyalties. It is common for parents to go from believing most teachers make wise decisions about homework and have students' best interests at heart to doubting every teacher and the entire educational system. This may cause parents to relax homework rules, which rarely serves a useful purpose. If a parent becomes convinced that schools or teachers are sorely lacking, he may wish to become more involved in working to change them. As far as the child's studying goes, parents should ask themselves which is worse: enforcing study sessions so the child can complete questionable homework assignments or abandoning studying altogether?

It is important for parents to remember that there is a difference between "sympathetic words" and "sympathetic actions." While children are helped by the former, parents who change rules or fail to enforce limits because they sympathize with a child's plight can do quite a bit of harm. "Since you're so tired, you don't need to do your homework," is not a constructive response.

★ *Children may need to view sympathy in a new light.* Some youngsters have learned over a period of many years that eliciting parental sympathy causes their parent to back down. Such children may become very frustrated when parents respond to their feelings but don't proceed to give in. Often they escalate their struggles. It may take a while to learn the "new rules" under which the parent is operating. Parents may speed up this process by saying, "In the past when I have been sympathetic, I have changed my rules. However, I know changing the rules is really not in your best interest. If I seem sympathetic, it is because I truly am. However, I shall not allow the rules to be changed, despite my sympathy."

Communicating on the Cognitive Level

The cognitive level is the level of the intellect. At this level, thoughts and knowledge are primary. When children communicate on the cognitive level, they tell about what they know or seek knowledge. When responding at this level, parents are likely to sound like teachers. Their communications are intended to provide information or expand children's knowledge. Cognitive conversations about homework typically occur in two situations.

1 When a child talks about why he should or shouldn't do his homework

2 When a child asks for information or help with the work itself.

The rule of thumb in discussing why children should do homework is this: *The less said the better.* Parents who spend much time on this subject are likely to waste their child's time — time that could be better spent studying, playing, or even watching T.V. Almost all cognitive discussions that center around why children must do homework are either irritating, boring, or counterproductive. Too often parents of children with homework problems spend inordinate amounts of time and energy telling children over and over again about why homework is important and why they must do it.

Given that a parent has delivered countless talks on the importance of doing homework with little effect, I recommend parents write out a lecture. The formal lecture must be introduced with an explanation. Otherwise the child may think he is hearing "the same old thing" and ignore the lesson. The opening remarks should get the child's attention, demonstrate your concern about the problems, and set a new tone for future communication about homework.

I recommend parents be somewhat dramatic as they deliver the lecture. Have the child sit at the kitchen table with paper and pencil for note-taking, while you read your speech. Children over the age of nine are likely to roll their eyes at these antics and say the whole procedure is "dumb," but they will be very impressed. They will listen.

Why Homework Is Important
by Mom and Dad

Most people think homework is important because it gives kids a chance to practice the school lessons they learned during the day. This is true, but it is only the beginning.

Homework teaches many things that students cannot learn in the classroom. Homework gives children an opportunity to solve problems on their own. In this way, they learn to use their own minds. When a student solves difficult problems without help, he feels proud and develops better self-esteem.

Doing homework regularly teaches responsibility. When children grow up they will be responsible for all areas of their life. Working, keeping up a house, and raising a family aren't so scary for those who have had lots of practice being responsible.

Setting aside study time each day teaches children to budget time and plan ahead. They get practice making choices about how to use their free time.

When a student completes all of the homework, including the work that seems too easy and the very hardest problems, he'll be able to face challenges. Many people never learn to do that. When they become bored or when things seem difficult, they quit. Later they may say, "I wish I hadn't quit that job. It was really a good one. I wish I had learned to stick with things."

Some homework assignments help children develop their creative abilities. When students choose their essay, term paper, or science project topic, they have a chance to consider what interests them.

Doing homework helps children make good grades, which is necessary for getting into college or getting good jobs. But, most important, getting a good education helps people to understand the world and to manage their lives.

A Helping Hand?

Another time at which parents typically respond at the cognitive level is when children request help with homework. A child asks a simple, straightforward question and awaits a response. Conscientious parents are prone to give a simple, straightforward answer in an attempt to help their child out. However, this is the point at which children are in danger of abdicating responsibility for doing their own work, and many a well-meaning parent falls into "the trap." Of course, it is easier on the child if the parent simply gives the correct spelling of "dinosaur" rather than handing him a dictionary! But learning to use a dictionary is a major academic skill.

Parents who simply provide the answer prevent their child from learning something much more important than the spelling of one word.

Similarly, when a child says, "I don't understand the directions on this homework paper," parents need to consider carefully before reading and explaining them. Doing so may deprive children of the opportunity to practice several other important study skills such as reading the directions, asking questions at the time the assignment is given, and learning how to figure things out on their own. Further, parents run the risk of supporting dependent behavior and undermining a major purpose of homework, which is for children to have an opportunity to solve problems themselves.

By providing indirect help rather than responding directly to requests for information and assistance with homework, parents can ensure they are providing for their youngster's long-term best interest. Methods of doing this are discussed in chapter 7, along with guidelines for providing direct help.

Communicating on the Behavioral Level

When communicating about behavior, discussions center around actions. This is the level at which homework struggles may become a bit nasty. A child communicating at this level tells what he is or is not doing. "I can't do my book report because I didn't finish the book," "I'll start my homework after the next commercial," "I'm working on Spanish," are examples of behavioral communication. Instead of speaking, the child may simply be doing something such as reading a magazine, staring out into space, or working on his homework. With or without words, children are always communicating.

In responding at the behavioral level, parents attend to children's actions. When parents communicate on this level, they often feel and sound like sergeants. They call in the troops, issue commands, confine youngsters to quarters, conduct trials, and impose martial law. As in cognitive and emotional discussions, there are two types of responses: constructive responses which decrease power struggles and destructive ones which escalate them. Constructive responses occur when parents talk in a calm, respectful manner about the behavior and set clear, firm limits. Ordering, nagging, punishing and threatening are classified as destructive responses, because they cause children to feel angry, humiliated, frightened, or hurt.

Destructive Behavioral Responses

Although nagging, ordering, threatening, or punishing may bring about a temporary improvement in behavior, they increase the likelihood that children will engage in overt or covert power struggles. Many children are compliant at home because they are afraid of their parents, but act out their anger in other environments. A vicious cycle quickly develops: parents react punitively to try to control behavior at home; the child acts out elsewhere; the parent punishes the child for misbehaving; the child acts out even more. Abused children provide the best example of this. While some are meek and compliant at home, most are angry and rebellious at school.

■ **Nagging.** Nagging occurs when a parent continually tells or reminds a child to do something, but fails to provide sufficient limits to ensure compliance. Most parents find nagging a tedious and irritating affair, as do the children. Children typically respond by promising to comply but failing to follow through. Some tune the parent out altogether.

Parents continue to nag because they are uncomfortable asserting themselves or are unsure as to how to do so. Of course, some parents are chronic naggers who focus on their children's wayward behavior to relieve tension arising from other sources. Continued focusing on a child's deficiencies may be symptomatic of problems within the parent rather than the child. When a child complains that a parent is always on him about something, it is usually a signal that the parent is projecting his own problems onto the child.

■ **Ordering.** In ordering, parents tell a child what to do or how to behave in a manner the child perceives as thoughtless or humiliating. As with responses that are critical or blaming, there is no objective way to determine whether or not a response sounds like an order. At issue is the child's reaction to and feelings about the parent's statement, not how the parent meant to sound. The child's age often plays a role in his reaction. "Go do your homework" may not carry negative connotations to a third grader, but most teenagers feel demeaned by such a statement. The presence of friends or siblings also affects children's reactions. Even second grade children feel humiliated when parents issue orders in front of their peers or siblings.

■ **Threatening.** Examples of threatening responses are: "If you don't get busy now, I'll..."; "If you ask me one more question, I'll..."; "If you don't bring your assignments home tomorrow night, I'll..." Since parents are almost always angry when they issue threats, they often say things they do not mean or promise punishments they cannot deliver. Children learn to tune out parents who continually threaten. One positive outcome of threats is that they enable parents to vent their frustrations and may even result in a transitory improvement in the child's behavior. Threats do little to solve homework problems in the long run, and typically result in other problems.

■ **Punishing.** Punishing occurs when parents act on threats. They may withhold a privilege or carry out an action which is humiliating or hurtful to the child, such as washing his mouth out with soap or confining him in his room. Many parents use punishment in hopes of teaching their children respect. In actuality, punishment creates fear, causes youngsters to feel humiliated, and encourages them to hone their skills at manipulation to avoid being punished. It is only by being treated respectfully that children learn to respect others. Many parents confuse discipline and punishment. Discipline, which is derived from the word disciple, involves teaching. Disciplining children need not create fear or cause feelings of humiliation. Neither does it involve physical or emotional pain.

■ **A special warning.** Punitive approaches are not only ineffective for the above reasons, they carry an element of risk. It is a sad fact of modern life that parents must be very careful when punishing or even threatening children who are compliant and anxious to please. Suicide is now the second leading cause of death among children ages 12-18. (The first is accidents, but many "accidents" are masked suicides.) Many youngsters who tried to fulfill expectations for academic achievement have killed themselves rather than face parental disapproval or punishment. One thirteen-year-old shot himself after receiving a report card containing A's, B's, and a C. Before he left for school on report card day, his mother had said, "If your grades have gotten worse, you'd better not show your face around here again." His grade in health had slipped from a B to a C. He didn't ever show his face at home again.

In reality this child's parents had not been harsh or particularly demanding in their treatment of him and he had no reason to believe he would actually be disowned over a poor grade. In fact, he was a "homework fanatic." The pressures this compulsive studier placed on himself to achieve were largely internal rather than a reaction to pressures from parents. Yet when the external pressure was added to the tremendous strain under which he operated, it proved to be too much. The moral of this and countless other tragic stories is that sensitive, compliant children age 12 and older must truly be treated with "kid" gloves.

Constructive Behavioral Responses

Specific methods for setting and enforcing limits to teach good study habits and a responsible approach to doing homework will be discussed in the next chapter. To respond productively and reduce the potential for power struggles, parents must remain polite and respectful when responding to behavior. To do this, they are to lavishly employ the following "Common Courtesy" expressions:

★ "Please"

★ "Thank-you"

★ "I'd appreciate it if..."

★ "Would you mind...?"

★ "Excuse me"

★ "I'm sorry"

★ "I beg your pardon"

★ "I guess I was wrong"

★ "If I'm not mistaken..."

Below, constructive and destructive responses to children's behavior are compared. It often takes parents longer to formulate a constructive response, until the responses have become habits. Nevertheless, the reduction in power struggles results in a major savings of time and energy for busy parents.

Constructive: It's 7:00, which is the time we agreed you would begin your homework.
Destructive: (Ordering) Start your homework now!

Constructive: Please ask your friends to go home and gather your study materials.
Destructive: (Threatening) If you don't get your things and get busy, you'll have to sit here all night!

Constructive: I'm sorry, but to make up for that interruption, I must add 5 minutes onto your study period.
Destructive: (Punishing) That's it! You're grounded!

Constructive:	I'd appreciate it if you would ask your teacher about that before you leave school.
Destructive:	(Nagging) I've told you time and again to ask your teacher.

Winning the Homework Wars

Most children stop engaging in power struggles soon after parents eliminate destructive responses and substitute constructive ones. I know a few children who became completely self-motivated after parents altered their customary method of responding and reopened channels of communication that had been closed for several years. However, these children are the exception, not the rule. Most youngsters lack the maturity necessary to be consistently self-motivated. They need the concrete assistance of a study program, as outlined in the next few chapters.

Although the best offensive weapons in parents' arsenals are consistency and firmness, their strategic weapons are respect and kindness. Love expressed through warmth, acceptance, and unconditional positive regard are the most potent forms of ammunition for taking the "power" out of homework struggles.

Chapter 5

Setting the Stage for Studying

"Time to start your homework," Mrs. Jackson reminds Johnny.

"Oh, I don't have any homework tonight," Johnny answers, his clear brown eyes exuding truth and innocence. "I did it in school."

Across the street, in the Smith household, the evening interrogation begins. "Don't you have a book report due tomorrow?" Mrs. Smith queries Jane.

Jane is cool as a cucumber as she tosses out her reply. "The teacher postponed it. The report isn't due 'til next week."

Meanwhile, Mr. Reilly has been trying to keep up with his son's school work by talking to the teachers regularly. "But surely you have some math to do. Your math teacher told me he assigns homework every night," he insists when Sam denies having homework for the third night in a row.

"But he doesn't grade anything. He said he doesn't care what we do as long as we know how to work the problems," says Sam.

These parents are making heroic efforts to fight the homework war. They are concerned. They are involved. They are conscientious. They are not overly harsh or critical of their children. Nor are they permissive parents. But the homework war drags on and on. And everyone is losing.

These youngsters are not bad kids. They love their parents. They are generally well-behaved. They want to please and do well in school. They are not lying, just deleting a few facts. Here is the rest of their stories:

Johnny did do his science homework when the teacher provided his class with free time in school. But there's this little matter of an English essay he's supposed to write. Johnny is an optimistic, happy child who believes in the power of positive thinking. He's good at putting negative thoughts out of his mind. To Johnny, an English essay is a negative thought. He's already put it out of his mind!

Jane isn't lying, either. She's just withholding a bit of information. Although her written book report is due tomorrow, her oral presentation is a week away. Jane's teacher permits students to hand in late papers, although she does lower their grades. Jane has every intention of doing her written report and turning it in...later.

Sam is telling the truth, the whole truth, and nothing but the truth. His teacher doesn't grade math homework. The math teacher did tell the students they need not do the homework, if they know how to do the problems. Of course, Sam doesn't know how to work the problems, but he isn't aware of that fact. How could he overlook this little detail? He hasn't been doing his homework, so he doesn't know what he can and cannot do!

Getting children to complete daily school assignments and occasional long-range projects is not enough. *To win the homework war, parents need to institute a study program, not just a homework program.*

This is an important difference.

Setting up a study program as opposed to a homework program eliminates arguments of the "I-don't-have-any-homework" or "I-already-did-it-at-school" variety. A child's need to do homework on any given night may be debated endlessly; when it comes to his need to study there is nothing to discuss. All students benefit from studying. Therefore, this homework program requires parents to decide that their child needs to study every day and to institute a daily home study program to meet this need.

Parents who only require youngsters to study when homework has been assigned end up conducting covert operations in which countless hours are spent interrogating children and prying information from busy teachers to discover what is due when. Still, time and time again their intelligence network proves inadequate.

Even if parents were able to hone their spy tactics to the point that they could accurately determine exactly when a child had homework due and when every quiz and test were scheduled, I believe it is wrong for parents to do so. *It is the child's job, not the parent's, to keep track of school schedules.* Of course, if parents who have borne this burden suddenly drop the ball, their youngsters may not leap to pick it up. *A child will not learn to accept responsibility for such matters as long as someone else is doing it for him.*

The "learning to catch a ball" analogy is a good one. If every time a ball were thrown to your would-be all star, someone leapt forward to catch it for him, he would never develop the skills (concentrate, keep your eye on the ball, extend arms, open hands, step forward) necessary to succeed. Remembering when the next test will be held or the German project is due may seem like a simple task, but "remembering" is a learned skill. To master it, children must have the opportunity to practice, to make mistakes, and to be held accountable for those mistakes. Students may follow the form suggested for the "Student Assignment Notebook" in the Appendix to list assignments and study requirements. In so doing, they can employ organizational skills to compensate for difficulties memorizing and remembering...as soon as they remember to fill out the notebook in the first place!

An Overview of the Study Program

From the child's perspective, the study program is very straightforward. On Day 1 parents admit they haven't done enough in the past to help with studying and homework. They apologize to the child, beg forgiveness, and promise to do everything in their power to correct the situation by making sure the youngster has a chance to get his work done in the future.

On Day 2 parents call a family meeting and promise to provide daily study periods for problem studiers and a "quiet time" for the entire household. During this meeting parents solicit cooperation from other family members, describe the program, develop the study schedule, and work out miscellaneous details. Children being placed on the study program are given contracts to sign to ensure they understand what is expected of them.

On Day 3 the child has a study period, and the program is off and running. Ideally, all family members participate for the first two weeks. The parent continues to hold nightly study periods and provides close supervision until the child is established on the program (this usually takes about a month). Then, the parent begins reducing the amount of supervision until the child is working on his own.

Parents have a number of details to work out and decisions to make before the program can be implemented. The rest of this chapter takes parents through the preparatory steps.

The Peace Conference

Parents are to carefully set the stage for the program by shepherding youngsters who need help with homework to the conference table for an intergenerational summit. The goal is to obtain a cessation of hostilities and permanent cease fire. Parents are to arrive armed with an inspired speech containing hints of a treaty, a suggestion for disarmament, and a proposal for a new alliance as they make a major peace initiative.

Many parents do some crying as they carry out this step. Most children do, too. Some parents deliver their speech via a written note slipped under their child's bedroom door. This can work just as well or better than a direct talk, since most youngsters who hear the speech don't know how to respond anyway. If they have the speech in writing, they can re-read it several times. If the child is too young to read, parents can make a tape recorded message instead.

Even though I consider the passing of the peace pipe to be a preparation for implementing the full study program rather than the final solution, some parents of older teenagers have sworn their youngster's homework problems disappeared as soon as they completed this initial step. A 17-year-old boy told me, "When I read Dad's note, I finally realized he really is on my side. I guess I always thought he was punishing me or making a power play, when he'd hassle me about school and studying. When I first read the letter I didn't even think he wrote it: It was too out of character. I read it a couple more times and then I started crying. Things have just been so bad between us for so long. I'd always wished we could be close. Of course, a day later he was after me about stuff again, just like before. But it doesn't make me mad any more. Now I know what he's really trying to do. He only wants what's best for me." This boy's father said, "He's finally growing up so things are better now. I still don't believe in all this psychology stuff." The boy's mother later mailed in a check for the last counseling session with a one sentence note. It said, "Thank you for giving me my son back."

To set the stage for the new study program parents simply write a speech or letter in which they apologize for past errors and omissions and express determination to handle homework differently in the future. Here is a sample letter.

Dear Johnny,

In the past I don't think I've done a very good job of helping you be the best student you can be. I'm very sorry about this because I know it caused problems for you and affected your grades. I know it affected your sleep...remember the time we stayed up half the night getting you caught up on your book reports?

When we'd argue about you not doing your homework or studying, I'd sometimes yell at you and say mean things. I feel badly about the times I got mad when you asked for my help with homework, and I want to explain what was happening. When I didn't know how to help you, I couldn't admit that I didn't know what to do. So sometimes I got angry and treated you as if you weren't very smart or just weren't trying. I'm very sorry. I may not be a good teacher, but you certainly are not a dummy.

Now that I've read a book that teaches parents how to help their children with homework, I realize the many mistakes I've made. I realize that all you really needed all along was a regular time and a quiet place to study. I know it is normal for kids not to like to study after school — it's much more fun to relax after a long school day. And I know it's a parent's responsibility to make sure kids have time to do their work and review for school the next day.

That's a parent's duty, and I'm sorry I didn't do it sooner.

I promise to try harder to teach you what you need to know so you can become the best student possible. I hope this will help you at school. I'm sure it will help you in your life.

Sincerely,
Mom

I have never yet met a child who was able to remain angry in the face of a pure, unadulterated parental apology. Sometimes it is hard for parents to keep the apologies "unadulterated" though, and they sneak in a few lines here and there in which they project blame and cast criticism. Examples of adulterated apologies are: "...when you put your science project off to the last minute even though you had plenty of warning and then expected me to bail you out at the last minute..." or "...when you'd beg for my help and then dump all the work on me..." or "when you lied all semester long about having homework and I finally caught you..." These apologies have been contaminated with sprinkles of blame which dilute the main point and destroy the flavor of the message. Remember that the point is to apologize for your personal errors and omissions to set a new tone for homework, not to complain about your child's failings.

It takes a very big person to apologize. The best thing about apologizing to a child is that he has a chance to learn first-hand that a heartfelt "I'm sorry" can be a potent instrument for soothing hurt feelings, resolving conflict, and paving the road toward change. Once a child has experienced this magic, admitting his own shortcomings becomes easier. Then forgiving becomes easier, too.

Who Should Be Placed on the Study Program?

Children who are having problems studying regularly and/or completing their homework can benefit from the study program. Since a parent must supervise and the entire family must observe quiet time so as not to disturb those who are working, it usually makes sense to encourage all school-aged children to participate. Even primary school students who are not yet bringing home assignments can participate by spending study periods looking at library books, coloring, doing puzzles, or engaging in another quiet activity.

Some primary school children may actually need a study program to correct problems. One mother of a kindergarten student received a call from the teacher asking why the youngster hadn't been turning in assignments. "Why didn't you tell me you had homework to do?" the mother later asked her child. "Because you'd make me do it!" came the reply. While the merits of assigning homework to little ones may be debated, parents who set aside ten to fifteen minutes each evening during which the child is expected to sit quietly and color, look at books, or complete small tasks can help establish studying as a part of their daily routine.

When an older sibling is placed on the study program, younger siblings are usually amenable to participating whether they really need this extra structure or not. However, older children who are excellent students may balk at being required to attend formal study sessions simply because a younger brother or sister is having problems. In deciding whether or not to require an academic wizard to participate, parents should consider the following:

★ Does the student let work pile up for several days and then have to study for hours on end to catch up?

★ Does the student sometimes stay up so late cramming he is exhausted the next day?

★ Is the student's academic performance consistent? Or do his grades change dramatically from day to day, week to week, or semester to semester?

★ Does the student do well in all subjects or neglect some classes?

★ Does the student work independently, or does he frequently ask for help?

★ Does the student sometimes miss school because he hasn't finished a paper or isn't ready for a test?

★ Does the student know when to call it quits? Or does he obsess over details, tending to be perfectionistic and compulsive?

Even students who make excellent grades may benefit from the structure of this program. Many a high school valedictorian has been ushered into the hallowed halls of higher education, merit scholarship in hand, only to be ignominiously stripped of the honors and sent home a semester later. Students can thrive in many high schools on intelligence alone, but they cannot survive in college unless they study consistently. "Homework fanatics"who drive themselves to exhaustion may also benefit from the structure provided by this program.

Although you may decide not to require one or more of your children to participate in the study program, you should nevertheless extend an invitation to all family members, so they know they are welcome at the study table at any time. In many households, these study sessions become warm family gatherings, so it is important that no one be excluded. (Good feelings and warm fuzzies flowing around a study table during a homework session? Yes! It usually happens!)

Consider asking all family members to make a voluntary commitment to attend daily study sessions for the first two weeks to help get the program off the ground. Even if the others are coloring, building model airplanes, or playing solitaire at the study table, this demonstration of family support is most impressive to resistant studiers.

There are several good reasons to require siblings to participate for the first week or two. Since all family members will have to observe quiet time during the study periods, having everyone attend for the first week or two can help reduce interruptions. The supervising parent's job is much easier if everyone is in the same room, eliminating the need to run to other parts of the house to check on other children. Further, siblings are more apt to remember to observe quiet time after having attended sessions for a week or two.

Requiring siblings to do homework, read, or engage in an educational activity during study periods helps those who do have poor study habits. Too often poor students mistakenly believe themselves incapable of doing as well as siblings who are high achievers. If a good student always studies alone in a bedroom, the poorer student may not have had the opportunity to see his sibling engrossed in studying, and may not even know the secret of his success.

A personal example illustrates this point. In discussing this book with my brother, Bill, our conversation became personal as we shared childhood memories. "I was always jealous of you," Bill said, "I wished I had your brains. You never had to study and school was easy for you. How could I ever compete with a sister like that?"

I was astounded to hear his comment. As the IQ tests tell it, he is by far the brighter person. In fact, I did study. And I studied. And I studied. Believing that genius is 10 percent inspiration and 90 percent perspiration, I closed myself in my room with only my books for company and perspired away. Bill knew about the results of my efforts: He saw my A-studded report cards and heard about my occasional honors and awards. But since he was closed in his room (playing, not studying) and I was closed in mine (studying, not playing) he never witnessed my efforts.

Adolescents are often torn between their wish to be part of the family and their need to establish their independence. It is a big request to ask them to participate in study periods on behalf of a sibling who is having trouble with homework. It is even a bigger decision for them to say "yes," even though they may actually wish to do so. Requiring them to attend study periods for two weeks, and making attendance optional beyond that point is a way of saying, "As a member of this family, you must join in this united effort to solve a big family problem. However, you're growing up and are doing well enough in school to make your own decisions about when and where you study. You're welcome to spend the study period reading a magazine instead of doing homework if you prefer."

Although everyone is to participate during the first week or two of the study program, the needs of each child should be considered in deciding whether to require attendance after that point. Often parents try to be fair to their children by treating them all equally, thus inadvertently denying each youngster's unique strengths and individual needs. There is no point in forcing a child who has very good study habits, is self-motivated, and is able to observe quiet time to participate in a program designed to teach good study habits to the unmotivated!

Parents should be tactful when communicating with their children so as not to humiliate the child who needs the study program. When presenting the study program to the family say, "Your brother needs help learning to do homework and study regularly. You don't need this help: Somehow you have learned to study without my having taught you. Now that I am starting a study program to teach your brother, I would like you to attend for two weeks to help show him how you do it. His academic future is at stake. I know that even though the two of you sometimes don't get along, when the chips are down you come through for one another. I know this is quite an imposition, but we need to all sit down at the same time for the next two weeks."

Respond to grumbles by saying, "Yes, it is a big sacrifice. If you don't want to use the study period to do homework, you may work quietly at the study table on something else. I plan to pay bills, catch up on paper work, write letters, read magazines, and work crossword puzzles."

If you decide to exempt one or more youngsters from the study program, respond to complaints from those who must participate by saying, "Yes, it does seem unfair. Your brother doesn't have to participate, because he learned to study and do homework long ago. Please forgive me for waiting so long to teach you."

When to Start the Program

This study program may be started at any time in a child's academic career from kindergarten through twelfth grade.

There is one important rule for determining when to start the study program: One parent must be present to supervise. During the first two weeks the child is on the program an adult must be available every evening all evening long. During the second two weeks an adult must be available for about twice the length of the study period. (If a child's study period lasts an hour, the parent needs to be available for two hours.) For the next two weeks, a parent should be available for the length of the study period, which may be as long as an hour for older children. However, since most youngsters are quite self-motivated by that point, a parent need not do much more than announce the start of the study period.

These time requirements pose a difficult sacrifice for parents who travel, who work evening shifts, have two jobs, or have evening meetings to attend. The study program should not be started until arrangements have been made to ensure that at least one parent can be available every evening for the first month. Another alternative may be to plan to hold study periods in the morning, before school. If being available to your youngster seems impossible, consider that if your child had a medical emergency, you would manage to cancel other plans to be there. Education is almost as crucial as health for adjustment and future well-being. Therefore, your youngster's need for your presence is truly an emergency. Be there!

Selecting a Location

In most households, children are sent to their bedrooms to study. This makes it virtually impossible for parents to supervise their activities. Many children resist being isolated from the rest of the family anyway. The isolation is even harder for children, if the parents' work schedules afford little time to spend together. Therefore, parents are to avoid conducting study periods in the child's bedroom, unless the parents are willing to spend the entire session in the bedroom, too.

It is important that a central location be chosen containing a table, chair, and adequate lighting. The kitchen or dining room usually works best, since busy parents can still cook, clean, and attend to younger siblings while supervising studiers (in the latter stages of the study program). Some parents prefer the living room, den, or library. As long as a table, chair, light, and a parent are present, these rooms can work quite well.

Time Requirements

The best way to determine the length of the study period is to survey teachers to find out how much time they recommend. A sample survey for soliciting this and other relevant information is provided in the Appendix. If teachers won't complete the survey, try getting the information over the telephone. If one or more teachers fail to return your call, contact the principal. Educators frequently complain about the lack of parental involvement and concern. If teachers don't cooperate, let the principal know that you're concerned and trying to get involved. If you still don't get a response, write a letter to the school board. If you still don't get results, threaten to run for the school board!

In the absence of guidelines from teachers, parents have to make the decision themselves. *Most parents require study periods which are much too long.* Because students with study problems have taken so long getting started, interrupted previous study sessions so many times, and failed to study at all on so many days, past homework sessions may have lasted many hours. If a child begins working immediately, does not interrupt the session, uses the time wisely, and studies every evening, much less time is required.

Below are guidelines for parents who are unable to get solid information from teachers. These guidelines don't take into account those children with special learning problems who may take longer than most children to complete work, or schools where educational standards are higher and students receive longer and more difficult assignments. Further, these guidelines assume study periods are being held Monday through Thursday and once on the weekend. Children who do not study on weekends may need to spend a bit longer each day.

Grade	Minutes
First	15
Second	20
Third	25
Fourth	30
Fifth	35
Sixth	40
Seventh & Eighth	45
High School	60

It may seem contradictory to encourage parents to err on the side of requiring too little time rather than too much. Nevertheless, it seems to work out better if parents make the sessions too short rather than too long. If the time seems reasonable or even brief to children, they are more likely to cooperate. Further, once youngsters are actually using their time to study, they usually continue working even after the period has officially ended. Few parents anticipate this; they are convinced their lackadaisical offspring are incapable of such self-motivation. Their shock is so great when their child says, "Just a minute, I'm not done yet," many parents fear for their health. "I just about fainted when he said he needed more time!" said one. "My heart skipped a beat," said another.

The other reason for requiring short sessions rather than long ones is that children have very short attention spans, so they may not derive much benefit from longer study periods. Even college students begin shifting about in their chairs and looking at the clock after 45 minutes of a lecture. Parents may divide sessions in half and offer a break in between, if they so desire.

If a child still has work to do even though his allotted time is up, he may continue to study "on his own time," either at the central study table or in the quiet of his bedroom. Studying that occurs above and beyond the required study period is left to the discretion of the individual child. However, the time should not be deducted from the next day's study period, unless prior arrangements have been made.

Scheduling Study Times

In many households, study sessions have to be scheduled at different times on different days of the week, since families have other commitments and activities that must be considered. For instance, it may be that to hold a 45-minute session on Monday nights, the study period has to start at 6:15 and end at 7:00, so as not to conflict with soccer practice, piano lessons, dinner, someone's favorite television show, or bedtime. On Tuesday nights, children may have to study from 8:15 to 9:00 because mother works late, father has a Rotary Club meeting, and the youngest child must be in bed by 9:15. Hopefully, the schedule can be arranged so that children always have a set schedule for each particular day of the week, that is, every Monday is the same, every Tuesday is the same, and so forth. If not, I recommend the use of a "month at a glance" calendar to write down the schedule for the entire month. It is important for parents to remember that children do not share an adult concept of time, and cannot be expected to remember complex timetables they can barely comprehend.

In the majority of households, participants in the program have to study concurrently. Otherwise, parents end up devoting their entire evening to supervising. Children who have shorter study periods may be allowed to begin at a later time than those who have longer ones, or may be excused from the study table when their time is up. They are still to observe quiet time as long as other children are studying. When the last studier's session is over, quiet time ends and other household activities may resume.

Since a parent has to be available to supervise until each child is well-established on the program, the schedule must reflect parents' needs rather than children's wishes. Nevertheless, it is important to take children's preferences and responsibilities into account as much as possible, and to include the children in the process of working out a timetable, even though the family is so busy the schedule virtually speaks for itself. Involving the studiers allows them to think about their learning style, personal preferences, develop problem-solving skills, negotiate, make choices, and confront realities. Since other family members will also be affected — given their need to observe quiet time — all family members should be present when scheduling is discussed. Adolescents are much more cooperative if their feelings are taken into account, as are younger ones who are old enough to have opinions. Studies show people to be more likely to cooperate with new policies, procedures and programs, if they have been included in the decision-making process.

Material Requirements

Only two items are needed: a timer for each studier and a clock for the parent. Timers should have an alarm and should be clearly marked or different enough so it is easy to tell which timer belongs to which child. Since parents extend the study period by several minutes to make up for interruptions, it is important to obtain timers that are easy to reset. Wind-up timers used for baking usually work best.

Next, parents must make a decision about whether to provide study materials in the event the child actually has no homework or has homework but doesn't bring any school books home. Some parents wish to allow children to read books or magazines for pleasure in this situation, since at least they are practicing reading. Such reading is beneficial to developing student motivation and improving the most important skill needed for academic success. Further, it upsets many parents to see their children just sitting and doing nothing. However, allowing free reading carries an element of risk, since some children would be happy to read stories for pleasure during every study period, thereby avoiding doing school work. It may be more effective to disallow anything but school materials.

Many children are so forgetful that just as they don't bring books and assignments home at night, they don't remember to take pencils and paper to class during the day. As they learn to think ahead and gather materials before each study session, they are acquiring an important skill. But how best to help them master it? One possibility is for parents not to make any special effort to provide supplies and simply let the child work it out. This may mean the studier has to get up several times to retrieve supplies. Since every time a child interrupts the study period the session is to be extended, he will soon be motivated to remember to bring his materials to the study table at the start of the session. This technique works quite well for helping children develop the skills of planning ahead and "remembering."

Some youngsters who lack organizational skills may benefit from more concrete help to learn to organize their materials so they can find them in the first place. Such children often have very messy rooms, school desks and lockers crammed with heaps of paper, and are lucky to find a matching pair of socks in the morning, much less their science notebook. For these children, parents may fill a fairly large cardboard box with commonly needed supplies such as colored pencils, magic markers, spiral binders, folders, erasers, pens, lead pencils, several kinds of paper, tape, scissors, hole punchers, protractors, compasses, rulers, a calculator, paper clips, pencil sharpeners, paste, glue, and dictionaries.

If the parent works to gather the supplies, purchases a few new items, puts them in a box and gives it to the child as a present to be used during study periods, this can establish a positive tone for the study program. It can be yet another way of saying, "I'm not placing you on this program to punish you. This is a partnership and I'm participating, too."

Rules For Studiers

Studiers on this program are to adhere to the following rules:

1. The study period is to begin exactly at the agreed upon time.

2. A timer announces via a buzzer when the study period has ended.

3. Quiet time must be observed until everyone on the study program has completed the study period.

4. Sleeping, doodling, and talking during a study period are prohibited.

5. Arrangements must be made at least 24 hours in advance to change the regular time of the study period.

6. If studiers need help with homework, they are to seek it before or after the study period or during breaks scheduled for this purpose.

Parents may add other rules before the program starts or after it has been implemented to take care of problems that arise. Remember that the fewer the rules, the easier it is for children to remember and follow them.

Rules for the Supervising Parent

Rules for the parent who is supervising the program are a bit more complex.

1. Announce one and only one time that the study period is about to begin, then immediately set the timer so the alarm will sound at the end of the session.

2. Time each interruption.

3. Immediately add the time lost during the interruption (one minute minimum; fractions of a minute should be rounded *up* to the next larger minute). Also, add an additional two minutes per interruption

onto the study period.

4 Reset the alarm on the timer to compensate the studier for the time lost due to interruptions.

5 Keep the household quiet and free from distractions.

6 Announce the end of quiet time.

7 Refrain from criticizing, blaming, arguing, or struggling in any way.

8 Retain the right to allow or disallow changes in the study schedule.

9 Complete the *Daily Progress Journal for Parents*.

Some examples illustrating how to time interruptions are given below:

Example 1

Interruption:	Door bell rings; child looks up.
Time:	30 seconds (round to 1 minute)
Add to timer:	3 minutes (interruption + 2 minutes)

Example 2

Interruption:	Child asks a question
Time:	1 minute, 15 seconds (round to 2 minutes)
Add to timer:	4 minutes (interruption + 2 minutes)

Example 3

Interruption:	Supervising parent must leave the room.
Time:	3 minutes, 4 seconds (round to 4 minutes)
Add to timer:	6 minutes (interruption + 2 minutes)

The additional two minutes is not a penalty! It takes into account the fact that people need a few moments to reorient themselves to a task once their concentration has been broken. Consider that if you are reading a book and the telephone rings, when you return to your book it takes a few moments to get going again. You have to pick up the book, open it to the right page, find your place, and reread a few sentences before continuing on. The additional two minutes is to compensate the child, and should therefore be referred to as "compensation time."

It is imperative that parents be clear within their own minds as to why they are providing additional time. Remember the goal is to protect your child's study time! Respond to complaints by saying, "I won't let you get cheated out of your study time! I won't cheat you out of it, I won't let your brother cheat you out of it, I won't let you cheat yourself! I won't let anyone take your study time away from you for any reason!"

Every time a parent adds minutes to the timer, he is sacrificing his own time and giving his child a gift. While children may not be grateful for this particular present, parents should not fall into the trap of believing they are meting out penalties or punishments. The goal is simply to ensure the child has time to study.

■ **Questions.** The regular study period is the child's time to study independently. Parents who want to provide time for the youngster to ask questions should do so by providing breaks designed for that purpose.

If you decide to allow breaks so studiers can ask questions, set the alarm to ring during the session. When it rings, query the child to determine if he has any questions. Reset the timer after you have finished helping, and repeat this process at the next scheduled break. *Time spent on breaks is not to be counted as part of the regular study period. The study period should be designated as the student's time to work on his own.* The recommended lengths for study periods do not take into account time spent tutoring, teaching, or helping. Therefore, if a child with a 20-minute study period spends 5 minutes getting help during breaks, his study period takes 25 minutes to complete.

Parents who provide helping breaks during which children may ask questions are encouraged to solicit their children's input as to when they want to schedule them. Some children prefer a break close to the beginning of the session to ask questions about directions; others prefer it close to the end so parents can look over their work.

■ **Quiet time.** Keep the household quiet and free from distractions. The T.V. and radio should be off, the telephone answering machine should be on (or callers should be asked to phone back later), and the entire family should observe a quiet time. Any time the studier is interrupted for any reason (a toddler starts crying and the studier looks up, a sibling speaks to the studier, a spouse gets home from work), the supervising parent is to add time to the study period (at least one minute for each interruption plus two minutes compensation).

Parents who continue to view the adding of time as a punishment may see this procedure as cruel. It is important to remember that you are not punishing your child for putting down his materials and spending a few moments greeting his father or for talking to a sibling! You are merely ensuring that such events do not deprive him of his study time. Pausing to greet father is important! However, every interruption means that studiers need a few moments to settle in again before they can resume studying.

Note that although the parent is responsible for controlling extraneous distractions such as the T.V., radio, infants, and toddlers, parents are not omnipotent and interruptions will occur. The telephone will ring. Friends will come to the door. Siblings will require attention. Life will continue to be predictably unpredictable. Supervising parents should attempt to eliminate as many external interruptions as possible while remembering it is impossible to prevent them all.

Announce the end of quiet time when the last studier's alarm has sounded. Allow the household to return to normal when everyone has completed the study period. Studiers who still have work to complete should be allowed to continue studying if they wish to do so. Since the house may now be noisy, studiers may prefer to finish up in their bedrooms. However, if they wish to remain at the study table or even finish up in front of the television, they should be allowed to do so. The possible exception to this would be setting limits on compulsive studiers.

■ **Avoiding conflict.** Refrain from criticizing, blaming, arguing, or struggling with children in any way. Simply time comments and complaints to determine how much time to add to the study period. Limit verbal responses to saying, "I'll be happy to discuss that with you after your study period has ended."

Retain your right to allow or disallow changes in the study schedule. In the event that a conflict arises (a PTA open house or choir practice is scheduled during the child's study period), it may be necessary to change the schedule for an evening. It usually is best to hold the study period before or after the special activity. If this is not possible, have the studier submit a plan for making up the time. Thus, a child may make up a thirty minute study period by studying ten extra minutes for three days, or fifteen extra minutes the day before and the day after the special event.

Insist that every missed moment of study time be made up! After all, if you permit your child to miss a study session because you have a club meeting to attend, why not let him miss to attend his club meeting with friends in the backyard tree house? If he must miss studying to attend basketball practice, why not let him miss because he has to watch T.V. or go out on a date with his girlfriend? If he has to miss because you have had something urgent come up, why not let him miss because he has had something urgent come up?

It's fine to change the scheduled times (with 24-hour notice) when special circumstances arise, but don't shorten the total time for any given week. If the child is simply too ill to study, double study periods as soon as he is feeling better. After all, there will be make-up work to complete.

■ **Falling asleep.** Awaken a youngster who falls asleep during a study period, send him to his bedroom to nap (if the study period is being held before dinner), or send him to bed for the night (if it is after dinner). The rest of the study period for that particular day should be canceled and an earlier bedtime arranged. The earlier bedtime should remain in force for the rest of the semester, unless the parent knows the child is exceptionally tired due to a special situation that interfered with bedtime or sleep the night before.

When setting a new, earlier bedtime, the parent should say, "I'm sorry, I didn't realize I set your bedtime too late for you to get enough sleep. That may be a part of what has made it difficult for you to do your homework and study. A parent's job is to make sure children get enough rest by setting reasonable bedtimes. We'll move up your bedtime by 15 minutes to see if that is enough to do the job."

Hold to the earlier bedtime! It really is a parent's duty to ensure children have a chance to get enough sleep! The only reason not to hold to the earlier bedtime would be if you later discovered your child's sleepiness was due to illness.

■ **Doodling.** Prohibit doodling during a study period. Immediately remove pencils, pens, paper and other school supplies, leaving only books and assignment sheets, saying, "I'm sorry, but this time is for studying only." Children can then spend the rest of their study session reading their books or staring out into space. They have the option to complete written work after the study period has ended or forego it altogether until the next day's study period. Don't offer second chances by collecting and returning materials during the same study session. Parents who do this discover that although children may not resume doodling, they continue attempting to manipulate the situation by engaging in another counterproductive activity.

Spend as much time as possible sitting at the study table. Read, write letters, pay bills, knit, or engage in another quiet activity. Being physically close not only allows for careful monitoring, but provides positive reinforcement as well. Parents who haven't the time to actually sit at the table must at least be in the same room, keeping track of interruptions until the child is established on the program.

Parents can gradually begin phasing out the program, giving their child more autonomy and control over the location and times of his study period. Allow your child to study without supervision after he is established on the program. Guidelines for accomplishing this transition are provided in chapter 6.

Rules to Avoid!

Note that there are no rules against staring out into space, tapping one's feet, fidgeting, or playing with lint. In fact, this is exactly what many children do during their first study periods, if they haven't brought home books and assignments. Just as you can lead a horse to water but can't make him drink, so you can lead a child to a study table but can't make him learn! Parents who try to penalize children for "not working" quickly find themselves in the midst of a power struggle. "But I was doing something! I was thinking about what I just read," children are apt to declare. Repetitive foot tapping or finger drumming are commonly used expressions of passive resistance and defiance among hostages, convicts, and children chained to study tables. Such behaviors are most irritating and upsetting to prison guards intent on maintaining control, breaking spirits and destroying morale.

This program does not call upon parents to act as prison guards. Therefore, foot tapping, finger drumming, bubble gum popping, giggling, fidgeting, pencil dropping, passing gas, and coughing are allowed. They are often methods of expressing anger or testing limits. Parents are urged to control their irritation by focusing their attention on studiously ignoring such behaviors. Parents can turn on a walkman to drown out upsetting noises. Remember that it takes two to have an argument! Ignoring such behaviors is the quickest route to making them go away.

Offensive behaviors that don't disappear over time are probably expressions of another problem. Fidgeting, finger drumming, foot-tapping, and bubble-gum popping are often expressions of nervousness and anxiety. Such behaviors serve to discharge tension and therefore may improve concentration. Fidgeting is also common among younger children who have less well-developed central nervous systems or those who have exceptionally high energy levels. It may require a lot of energy for such youngsters to refrain from fidgeting, thus interfering with their ability to study. Remember that you are establishing conditions to optimize your child's ability to concentrate, not yours!

Rules for Other Family Members

Siblings and other adults are to observe quiet time during study periods. Family members are to continue to observe quiet time even after the child is established on the study program by complying with the following rules:

★ Be quiet during the study period so as not to interrupt studiers.

★ If you must speak, do so in a whisper.

Each time another youngster interrupts the studier, the parent should whisper a gentle reprimand, such as, "Shhh...your brother has important work to do! You must be quiet so he can concentrate, remember?" Then time should be added onto the studier's study period.

Studiers who are in a hurry to complete their study period will quickly learn to ignore siblings who attempt to distract them. I highly recommend parents avoid jumping in the middle to try to control children's interactions.

It is not an issue of fault or blame. The studier lost some time; you are giving it back to him.

If the offender is another adult living in the house, it may be best to call a break and discuss the matter privately. Additional suggestions for controlling household distractions are presented in chapter 6.

The Study Contract

Children love to sign contracts. I'm not sure why they love it so much. Perhaps it makes them feel grown-up. Perhaps it helps them, just like adults, feel comforted and reassured by seeing exactly what the rules are and what is expected of them. On the next page is a sample study contract to be signed by those participating in the program. I have left space at the bottom for additional rules.

Other recommended rules include, "I must be quiet when other children are studying," and "If I need help with homework, I must ask for it before or after the study period" (or another variation developed according to recommendations for "helping breaks" outlined in chapter 6).

Communicating with Teachers about the Study Program

It is recommended that parents inform teachers that they are implementing a new study program. There are several reasons for notifying teachers. First, it is always important to let teachers know of events in your children's life that may affect their school work. Second, many teachers subscribe to the myth that students' academic problems are due to a lack of parental involvement. Informing them about your actions will let your child's teachers know that you are involved. This may offset their discouragement about having to "go it alone" and "care when no one else cares," thereby improving their attitude toward their job in general and your child in particular. Third, the quantity and quality of your child's academic work may change dramatically as soon as you implement this study program. It is important for teachers to receive enough information so they can understand what is happening. Fourth, if parents follow the suggestions for teaching problem-solving skills discussed in chapter 7, teachers will receive notes from home unlike those most teachers usually receive.

Summary

The most important point to remember is that you are working to solve problems not just for today, but forever. Despite parental fears that their

Student Study Contract

Beginning on _____(date), I understand that I am to
study _____minutes per night according to the schedule below:

Day	Beginning Time	Ending Time
Mondays	_____	_____
Tuesdays	_____	_____
Wednesdays	_____	_____
Thursdays	_____	_____
_____	_____	_____

I understand the following rules:

1 I will be notified ___ minutes before the study period is to begin.

2 I am not to sleep or doodle during my study period.

3 I am not to talk unless it is very urgent.

4 The buzzer will sound to let me know when my study period is over.

5 I must make arrangements one day in advance if I need to change my study period.

6 _____

_____

7 _____

_____

_____   _____
Date   Signature

child will just sit through study periods for the rest of his academic career without ever cracking open a school book, this is not what happens. Children may sit and stare for a day or two. Some may even sit with only their thoughts for company for the first six study periods. If parents hold firm, do not engage in power struggles, and are consistent for ten days, children get the picture: Study periods are here to stay. As soon as this reality sinks in, they grumble a bit less and resign themselves to their fate. And then they study.

Chapter 6

Implementing the Homework Program

Launching the Program

During a family meeting, the parent describes the study program, solicits children's recommendations for developing the study schedule, discusses rules for quiet time, and completes and signs study contracts.

It is important to present the program as a method for helping problem studiers rather than as a punishment, and to remain positive and non-judgmental regardless of the response from other family members. Allowing children to voice their complaints without trying to "sell them" on the program is the best way to avoid becoming embroiled in power struggles. If a child remains adamant about not wanting to participate in the study program, the parent may conclude the conversation by saying, (calmly! politely! respectfully!) "We'll give this program a try for a month and see what happens. I really believe it will help, and you may even find that you like it."

Here are the specific guidelines for presenting the study program to your family, soliciting their cooperation, and working out a study schedule.

■ **Complete copies of the *Study Contract* prior to the meeting.** If you are allowing breaks during which students may ask questions or if you have added other rules, be sure to note them in the contract.

■ **Give a copy of the *Study Contract* and *Quiet Time Contract* to each family member.** Even little ones who cannot read are to be included. Handing them a study contract communicates that they, too, are expected to pay attention and be involved.

■ **Announce the purpose of the new homework policies.** Be specific about the school, homework, study or achievement problems that demonstrate the need for a study program. Write out your remarks in advance, being careful to assume responsibility for past problems so as not to humiliate problem studiers or leave anyone feeling blamed or criticized. Read what you wrote aloud.

For example, say, "This meeting is to tell you about a new study program we will be having at home. I have been worried about your sister's school performance and have decided she needs more help to get her homework done. Every year her grades start out very good, then drop around Christmas. By the end of the year she is barely passing. She often forgets to bring her books and assignments home. These problems seem to stem from her difficulty doing her homework and studying regularly. After thinking about her situation, I realized I have never been consistent about ensuring she has enough time and a quiet place to do her homework and to study. I've decided the best thing to do is to start a study program for her. It begins tomorrow night, and I would like everyone to help her. It is a big sacrifice for all of us, but she is worth it. Really, her future is at stake." If more than one child is being placed on the study program, the parent describes the specific problems of each.

■ **Provide a brief description of the program.** Say, "Jill needs to study 30 minutes a day to make sure she has enough time to get her work done. She needs to study in the kitchen so I can make sure she gets the full time and isn't distracted by other activities or interruptions. During her study period, everyone else needs to observe quiet time. This means no one is to talk to Jill or me unless it's an emergency. If you come into the kitchen, you'll need to be very quiet. No one is to use the kitchen phone. The television, radio, and stereo are to be played softly so we can't hear it in here. Every time Jill is interrupted, I have to extend the session to be sure she doesn't miss any study time. So the fewer the interruptions, the sooner you'll be able to talk and play and watch television again.

■ **Solicit cooperation from other family members.** Say, "I really want all of us to pull together as a family to help Jill. I know everyone wants her to be the best student she can be. Here's how you can help. Jack, you've always been a good student. Even though I never took the time to teach you how to study, you managed to learn on your own. You can help by studying with us in the kitchen for the next week or so to show Jill how you do it. All you need to do is bring your books to the kitchen table and do your work in here, instead of in your bedroom. Joan, I need you to come, too, to show Jill we support her. Please join us at the study table during the study period for a week or so. You can bring a book to read or something else to work on quietly, such as your stamp collection. Baby Jason, every night I'm going to sit down with Jill while she studies, and you will need to be very quiet. You won't be able to talk to Jill during the study time, and you may only talk to me in a whisper. We'll bring some toys so you can play quietly in here, or you may play somewhere else. You'll have to be very quiet while Jill is studying." (Say this even though you suspect Baby Jason is too young to understand very much. First, he may understand more than you think. Second, it will impress Jill and other siblings that the issue is so urgent that even the youngest family members are being pressed into service.)

■ **Respond to complaints from other siblings in a non-judgmental manner and avoid being harsh or critical.** If the complaint is about having to participate ("I'm too busy," "I need to study in my room," "What's the point of sitting next to her and reading?") say, "Yes, it is a big sacrifice, but I need you to help," or, "It may be hard for you to see how sitting next to Jill and reading a book or studying will help her, but I am convinced it will." If the complaint involves criticism directed at Jill ("She's just lazy, she doesn't care about school"), defend Jill. Say, "I think the biggest problem is that we haven't worked together as a family to help her." If the complaint involves criticism directed at a parent ("You never make her do anything," "You do her work for her," "You let her get away with murder"), say, "I think I didn't know how to handle her study problems in the past, but I believe I now have a good plan and the will to carry it out." If the complaint involves criticism directed at the program ("She needs to study longer," "She doesn't need to study every day," "This won't help anything"), say, "I appreciate your concern. I'd like to start with this program. If things aren't better in a month, I would like to hear your suggestions."

■ **Feel free to press your children into attending if they decline to help out readily.** Having everyone together can make supervising much easier. It helps youngsters remember to observe quiet time after the week or two of mandatory participation is over. Say, "Jack, I realize you don't want to come to the study table because you usually talk to your friends on the telephone in the evening, but helping your sister is more important. For one week we need you to attend her study sessions. Bring a book to read if you don't want to do homework at the same time she does."

■ **If you decide not to require siblings to attend, leave the door open for them to support the program in the future.** Say, "All right, it sounds like you won't be available to help during the next week. But if at any time in the future you are at home and have the time, please consider bringing school work, a book, or something else to the study table to spend the session with Sally and me. It would really mean a lot to us."

■ **Begin developing the study schedule by querying each child placed on the program to determine his preference for study times.** Remember that since children are different, the time of day when they are most able to concentrate and perform academic tasks will vary. It is important for students to examine their individual preferences and learning styles, even if they cannot follow their inclinations due to family constraints.

Some students prefer to "hit the books" immediately after school while teacher's explanations are fresh in their minds. Some like to pause for a snack but study soon after they get home so they can "get it over with" and have the rest of the day to themselves. Others are more able to concentrate if they have an opportunity to relax and unwind before beginning homework, so they wish to postpone studying for an hour or so. Still others prefer to begin late in the evening when it is too late to go out and play. They have a hard time concentrating on school work if they know their friends are outside having fun.

I have met a number of early birds who claim to do their best work in the morning. They feel more confident taking quizzes and tests when they have studied in the morning. It is usually hard for parents to fathom this preference. Most are shocked to hear a youngster who rarely studies and who wages nightly battles over bedtime (striving to postpone it, of course) suddenly agreeing to go to bed a few minutes earlier so he can study in the morning. Yet when I have counseled families, many youngsters have proposed early morning study periods and have complied with earlier bedtimes.

If a child responds to your question about his preferred time to study by saying, "I want the study period to be at midnight!" or "I don't have a favorite time; I hate to study!" the parent should smile and nod and say, "I know. It would be more fun not to have to study at all. But if you did have to study, when would you prefer to do it?" (Parents should say, "if you did have to study" rather than "since you have to study," because the latter statement invites struggling.)

In the event that the child fails to state a preference, parents can usually assume they're up against a very resistant child and anticipate they're going to have a tough job ahead. Therefore, they should immediately solicit involvement from the rest of the family. It is harder for a child to resist in the face of a strongly united front of loving family members working to protect his best interests. The parent should say, "Your brother doesn't have a preference. What is the best time for the rest of you? Remember that everyone has to observe quiet time for 30 minutes a day, and I have to be here to supervise." Continue to provide openings as the conversation proceeds in hopes that the non-studier will get involved.

■ **If the child does state a preference, the parent should begin negotiating to develop a schedule.** The main interaction should be between the problem studier and the parent, with other children offering unsolicited advice from time to time. Before ending the discussion, the parent should make any remaining decisions that could not be settled by negotiation. For example, say, "We couldn't agree on when to hold the study period on Wednesday, so I am going to set the time that works out best for me: 7:00 p.m. We will begin at this time for four Wednesdays, and then we can talk about changing it if you wish.

Quickly review the final study schedule in light of the expressed preferences of each child. If the schedule fails to reflect the preferences of one or more studiers, comment on that fact. Say, "Jeff, you said at the beginning of this meeting that you prefer to study at night. Because we are such a busy family, we had to set a different schedule. As it stands, all of your study periods are scheduled for the morning. This worries me, because I think it would be better if you could study at the time that seems best to you. Unfortunately, I can't see a way to work out a better schedule at this time. We'll start with this one and follow it for four weeks. If it doesn't work out, we'll try to find a way to alter it.

■ **Beware of your own tendency to engage in power struggles!** It is often hard for parents to respond productively when their recalcitrant studiers suddenly defect from the enemy camp and try to participate in a family meeting. Parents tend to struggle as much or more than children when negotiating study schedules. Children often thwart the process by being silly and teasing one another at the outset, but as soon as they settle in, parents often thwart the process by discounting their proposals and arguing.

Most adults enter these negotiations convinced that if they ask, "At what time would you like to have your study periods?" the child will say, "Never!" When children respond positively, some parents overlook this victory and seek signs of the rebellious behavior and the negative attitudes they have so often seen in the past. In doing so, they may negate even straightforward replies. Once aware of this typical reaction, parents find it easier to avoid it.

Some examples may illustrate this point. When I mediated one meeting to help a family work out a schedule, the daughter said she wanted to start studying at 5:30 p.m. so she could visit her girlfriend after school for an hour and still finish homework in time for dinner. "You're just hoping I'll forget if I don't make you do it right away," her mother replied.

When working with another family, a father responded to his daughter's suggestion that she study at 4:00 by saying, "We already told you that you have to study when I can be home. You know I don't get home until 6:30. You're trying to avoid the issue."

During another family discussion a 10-year-old said, "I want to study before James gets up and turns on the stereo." It turned out his brother blasted the stereo from the moment he woke up until he went to sleep at night. To hear the words "I want to study" coming from the mouth of this particular child felt to me like a great victory. The father, however, was not impressed. He agreed that the stereo was a problem, but harshly criticized the youngster's proposal and overlooked the first sign of cooperation his son had ever shown. Discouraged parents are often their own worst enemies.

■ **Consider allowing problem studiers to withdraw from other activities to free up time for studying.** I have known many children who want to hold study periods during soccer practice or ballet lessons in hopes of being allowed to drop out of them. Parents are usually opposed to this: They want the child to continue other activities and schedule study sessions around them. My personal bias is that it is better to allow the student to drop such extracurricular activities even though I doubt the main motivation is to have more time to study. Any child who even suggests he would rather study than take ballet or attend soccer practice really wants out of the activity! Parents often worry the child may regret the decision in years to come; this study program, however, involves adding yet another structured activity to a child's life. Most children have too many structured activities and not enough time for free play to begin with.

■ **As you end the discussion, remind everyone that tomorrow is the big day for students who are beginning the program.** Say, "Be sure to bring school books home whether or not you have homework tomorrow, since you will have your first study period." *Post a completed copy of the contract on the refrigerator or in another easily accessible spot.* Write the daily study times on a calendar for the entire month so children can review it readily.

Remember that even if no one seems to be cooperating during the family discussion, you still have accomplished a number of important things. You have informed everyone about the program. You have explained how they can help problem studiers. You have given studiers a chance to identify their preferred times to study. You've established the study program as serious business and alerted everyone about what is expected of them. You have some idea of the level of resistance you will encounter, based on the cooperation you received while developing the study schedule.

A Word of Caution!

It is important for parents to examine their own values and attitudes toward their child's study time, because this program requires parents to extend the study period whenever the child is interrupted for any reason.

The purpose is to compensate him for the lost study time. It is not a question of who is to "fault" or "blame" for causing an interruption. Many interruptions are unavoidable, and are not necessarily "bad." A parent may be glad a child interrupts his studying to help out with a younger sibling, to answer the door, or to turn off the stove. When a parent extends the study period the intention is to protect the child's best interest, which is to have his full time to study! A parent who is able to sympathize with a child's feelings without becoming caught up in them can maintain an attitude that says, "I'm sorry you feel punished when required to study. However, I personally view your study time as a precious commodity. I will not allow anyone to rob you of it, not even other family members." Parents who are able to remain clear about their feelings, and kind and considerate when they act on them, may find their child adopts these attitudes and values.

Some parents are tempted to spend part of the child's study period teaching study skills, discussing school and study problems, or tutoring. I strongly recommend they pursue such activities before or after the study period rather than during it, or set up special breaks designed for this purpose. The suggested length of study periods is very short. Lines of responsibility become blurred when parents use their child's study time to teach, tutor, or talk. Study periods are the child's time to work independently and to learn to handle responsibility on his own.

Supervising the Study Program

Helping a child become established on a study program requires kindness and patience. The first goal for a resistant child is to get him to the study table. Once that is accomplished, children need time to deal with their feelings in order to become comfortable with the situation. This can take a while, since many children's basic dislike of homework is compounded by the fact that they have had bad experiences with it. Once the child has learned he will not be allowed to leave the table despite his refusal to do homework or study, boredom sets in. If he is still required to remain at the table and if others are busily working or reading, his boredom will lead him to open a book. If he receives acknowledgement and encouragement in the form of a smile for each small step toward studying he takes, his motivation to continue is increased.

It is possible that several days or even a week may pass during which the studier does nothing at all. Although a few days is very little time when the goal is to achieve a permanent solution, they may seem very long to parents who are worried about whether the child will ever use the time productively. Yet trying to speed the pace by hurrying the child actually slows down the process. Attempts to pressure and coerce increase the child's resistance.

Parents usually threaten, punish, order and nag when they are upset, and many do feel upset during the first few weeks the child is on the homework program. Parents are likely to feel frightened ("Will this program really work?"), irritated ("This is taking a lot of time and he doesn't appreciate my efforts"), frustrated ("I'm putting more energy into this than he is"), hopeless ("He'll never actually use his time to study"), and inadequate ("I'm not supposed to say or do the things I'm accustomed to saying and doing").

Despite the best laid plans, some parents find themselves losing control and reverting back to old behavior patterns. Parents who find themselves criticizing, blaming, nagging, ordering, threatening, or punishing should apologize, announce their need for a short break, and suggest the child take a break as well.

Parents should give some prior thought to how they may spend the break to regain their composure during this type of situation. It helps to have a list prepared in advance. When people are feeling overwhelmed, it is harder to develop workable solutions. Some parents spend their break walking around the block, closing themselves in the bathroom, talking to a spouse or friend, or even shredding phone books to relieve tension and vent frustrations.

The First Study Period

During the next month you should have ample opportunity to catch up on those magazines you've been wanting to read, the letters you've been meaning to write, the bills you've been needing to pay, or the craft project you never had time to finish. Gather such items, along with a pen or pencil and this book, placing them on the study table in a tidy stack. During the first few study periods, many parents are busy timing interruptions, resetting alarms, and filling out the Parent's Progress Journal (to be explained shortly). Have a stock of personal supplies ready anyway. It is important to demonstrate what is to be done before a study period: Gather materials and be ready to start on time. And who knows? Youngsters who are participating in the program just might spend the whole time studying from day one, siblings may remain quiet, and you'll actually have time for yourself!

If family members who are not participating in the program are at home, be sure to notify them that quiet time is starting. Say, "Johnny's study period is about to begin. Everyone must remember to observe quiet time. Johnny, it's 7:28. I'll be setting the timer in exactly two minutes." Again, it is important to sound cheerful and upbeat when announcing the study period. Try to avoid saying, "Time to do your homework," or repeating the same statements you have made in the past, as it invites your child to repeat his typical responses.

Parent's Progress Journal

As soon as the timer is set, sit down at the study table and write the time under item #1 of the Parent's Progress Journal located in the Appendix. During the first month your child is on the program, use this journal to record events that occur during the study periods. Completing this journal may seem like a nuisance, but it is important. Data from the journal serve three important functions.

1 It helps combat the normal tendency to overlook problem behaviors on days when a parent is feeling happy and in control, and to overreact when feeling down. The goal is for the parent to be consistent, not only in terms of holding sessions and following through with limits, but in terms of maintaining a positive attitude. Many children feel punished when required to attend study periods. When parents become frustrated or angry, they support the misperception that the study periods are a punishment.

2 With the journal parents focus on behaviors which may signal other difficulties the child is having. Many children whose aversion to homework appears to stem from laziness or disinterest actually have other problems, such as difficulties organizing their studies, budgeting time, concentrating, or feeling overwhelmed by the work. By focusing on specific behaviors, parents can develop hypotheses about underlying difficulties. However, it is not possible to reach definite conclusions by observing behavior. A parent who observes her child arriving late to study periods may conclude that he is angry about the sessions and rebelling, when in fact something else is preventing him from arriving on time. Therefore, parents must refrain from jumping to conclusions. Often they will not really know what caused a particular problem until it is solved. Observing behavior enables parents to make educated guesses about underlying problems.

3 The journal helps the parent track the child's progress. A child is established on the program when he meets the following criteria for ten consecutive study periods: He arrives on time to scheduled study periods after being called once; he spends the entire study period doing homework, studying, or pursuing another educational activity.

Time Study Period Started

In the first item of the Parent's Progress Journal, record the time at which you set the timer to begin the study period. If children are scheduled to begin their study periods at different times, write each youngster's name and note the time you set each timer. Under the section labeled "Grade," write a plus sign (+) for each child whose study session began on time and a minus (-) for those who began late. Note the reason for the tardiness under the column labeled "Comments."

■ **Typical Problems.** Getting children to show up for their study periods is the first problem many parents encounter. If your child disappears and claims to have lost track of time, buy him a watch. For less than $10.00 you can purchase a digital watch with a built-in alarm.

If a watch fails to remedy the problem, another solution will be required. Requiring the child to come directly home from school and to stay home until after the study period often works. If the same problem continues tell your child he must submit a written plan or prepare a talk explaining how he plans to prevent a recurrence of the problem. Here is a plan developed by an 11-year-old which the father deemed acceptable.

> *Coming Home To Study*
> *Next time I go out I'll say where I'm going so you can find me when it's my study period. If I go somewhere else I'll come home and tell you before I go there.*

When a parent approves a plan and it turns out not to work, many parents feel betrayed and they become angry or upset with the child. Sharing such feelings with the child is rarely productive. Since the adult approved the plan, he must accept responsibility for having accepted it.

I suggest parents have the child develop and submit a second plan, or simply provide him with one. One possibility is to require the youngster to come directly home after school every day for a week and remain in the house until the study period has ended each day. Do not present this as a punishment! Your child may feel punished, but your duty is to teach. Say, "You're continuing to have difficulties remembering to come home on time for your study period. I've been trying to think of a way to help you develop the habit of coming home on time. I think the best solution is for you to come directly home after school every day for a week and not go out until after your study period is finished. That may make it easier to remember in the future. After the week is up, you may again go outside after school and we'll see if you're able to remember to come in to study."

Minutes Late to Study Period

Even though everyone is at home and you set the timer at the scheduled time, children may still arrive late. They may pause to use the bathroom or gather supplies. They may stop off for a snack when you call them. To complete this item, write the number of minutes each child was tardy. In the column labeled "Grade" write a plus sign for each child who arrives on time and a minus sign for those who arrive late. Under the column labeled "Comments," note the reason for the tardiness. If you are the cause of a child's tardiness, write "ME" in the comments section.

There are unpleasant consequences for tardiness throughout life. At school, students receive detentions for arriving late to class. Employers fire employees who are chronically late. Arriving ten minutes late to an important meeting may spell disaster for even a high-ranking executive. It is important to teach your child to be on time!

■ **Typical Problems.** If you are chronically late, make a special effort to begin study periods on time, even though you continue to arrive late to other appointments. If a precocious child takes exception to your double standard, remind him that study periods are more important than most of your other obligations.

If the child is chronically late, providing a five- or ten- minute advance notice may help. Otherwise the parent should discuss the problem and ask if he can do anything to help the child arrive on time. This discussion should take place after the study period has ended. Discussing it at the outset serves to further delay the study period and may cause the child to feel upset, making it harder to concentrate on assignments.

Parents may provide a consequence when children are late to study periods. If you give your child an allowance on a regular basis, consider "docking his pay" a specified amount every time he is tardy. After all, this is what will happen if he arrives late to his job in the "real world." If you don't provide allowances, withhold another privilege such as watching television. Keep the consequences short and simple: "arrive late today, allowance reduce by 'x' amount this weekend," or "arrive late today, no television afterwards." Consequences should be presented as the parent's attempt to find ways to help the child remember and follow through with his responsibility. Consider the following parental responses:

Response #1. "I've been trying to think of a way to teach you how important it is to arrive to study periods on time. Those who don't learn to be on time end up with many problems: They get detentions at school, they lose their jobs, they disappoint their friends. Therefore, I must be sure I teach you. If you arrive late, you will have to go to your room after the study period and stay there until bedtime. I hope this will help you to think about the importance of arriving on time."

Response #2. "I can't believe you're late again! When are you ever going to show some respect? After your study period is over, you are to go to your room and stay there for the rest of the night!"

The parent in the first example sends the message that he is concerned and is trying to teach something important. The parent in the second example sends the message that he is angry.

Complaints

If a child moans and groans on the way to the study period or interrupts his session to complain, note it in the journal. If your child says, "But I don't have any homework!" "Do I have to?" "It's no fair," make a mark for each complaint under "Day" to tally the gripes. Keep track of barely audible grumbles, mumbles, groans, and non-verbal statements, too. Sometimes a grimace or roll of the eyeballs can say as much or more than words alone.

Complaints are the easiest study problem to deal with. If they are expressed immediately before a study period, be sympathetic or respond empathetically. Say, "I know, it's a bother, isn't it?" as you set the alarm, but don't delay setting it! If grumbles occur during the study period, time them (only the spoken complaints; you can't time a grimace!) and add the minutes spent complaining along with the two minute compensation time onto the end of the study period by resetting the alarm. Before you actually reset the alarm say the following: "Every time people interrupt themselves or break their concentration it takes a few minutes to get started again. Therefore, every time you complain about studying or interrupt your session, I add the time you spend talking plus two more minutes onto your study period. If you wish to discuss something, we can do it before or after your study period." Do not spend additional energy explaining, justifying, rationalizing, or excusing your actions. Just keep resetting the timer!

Remain unbending in your determination to refrain from arguing or discussing your policies. Simply reset the alarm to compensate for lost time. If your child says things you find unacceptable or hurtful, deal with these problems after the study period has ended. Do not take time out to try to resolve other problems, as this only serves to further delay the study period!

The accumulated data under "Comments" helps assess each studier's change in attitude toward studying. There are two common patterns. One is for studiers to be resistant to the study program initially, to improve after a few days, and to have a setback during the first study period after a weekend or extended holiday. When a child stops grumbling on Mondays and after school vacations, it is an indication that he is accepting the program. Combined with other positive signs (bringing books home, using the time to study, receiving good reports from teachers), parents have a basis for determining when the child is sufficiently established on the program to need less supervision.

Another common pattern is for children to be highly motivated and compliant at the outset of the program and then to become more resistant as the novelty wears off and the study periods become routine. Children who prefer the novel and become bored with the predictable often take a longer time to become established on the program.

Remember, however, that feelings and actions are two different things! *Children who continue to express their dislike of having to study may still be responsible studiers!* It is fine for youngsters to dislike studying, dread the sessions, and moan about them afterwards. Talking about feelings cannot hurt, and it may help. A child who complains before and after study periods but spends the time working is demonstrating considerable emotional maturity: He is able to express his feelings at appropriate times, yet keep his emotions from interfering with his work.

If a child who is well-established on the study program suddenly begins complaining about having to study and do homework again, it may be that a specific problem is creating the renewed discomfort. Use the problem-solving techniques discussed in chapter 7 to help identify and resolve it.

Brought Study Materials

If your child does not bring materials to the study table, allow him to retrieve them, but extend his study time according to the rules (time plus two minutes compensation). However, do not insist he bring work to the study table, as this is a way of trying to control the uncontrollable. Remember that you can lead a child to a study table, make him bring his books, but you still can't make him study!

Note whether each child arrives at the study table with some basic materials such as books, assignments, pens, pencils. This provides another measure of the child's ability to handle responsibility, ability to plan ahead, and/or ability to organize.

■ **Typical Problems.** Children who arrive empty-handed may be communicating, "You can make me attend a study period but you can't make me do anything!" "I can't think far enough ahead to get my books from my room before sitting down at the study table," or "I'm so disorganized I forgot my materials."

Information from this journal section helps parents determine what kind of corrective action is needed. Make a guess as to the source of the problem, noting it under "Comments." For example, write "planning problems," "poor organization" or "rebelling." Put a question mark after your note to remind yourself that this is a hunch rather than a definite conclusion.

If, after several days, your child is still arriving without assignments, try to identify the problem and take some action. That does not mean it is time to be critical and angry! Ask your child why he doesn't bring home his books and assignments; ask if there is anything you can do to help. Pose specific questions about what happens at the end of a school day. Children who are afraid of being reprimanded may be hesitant to talk, so parents must make an effort to express their desire to help. Here are some reasons children don't bring their work home:

1 They are afraid to take time out to go to their locker for fear of missing the school bus.

2 They don't want to go to their locker after school because another student bothers them.

3 Peers tease them about taking their books home to study and they don't know how to respond to save face.

4 The books are heavy and the child has a long walk home.

5 They have lost their locker combination, a stack of books, or a single book, and are afraid they'll get in trouble if parents and teachers find out.

These are specific, concrete problems which parents can usually find a way to solve. Although teachers are often willing to help by making sure the child has his books and assignments with him when he leaves school, I do not recommend this unless the child is very young (in primary school), is just beginning to receive assignments, or unless there is another compelling reason. Children do need to learn to be responsible for bringing home books and assignments. They will not learn if someone else assumes the responsibility for them.

Sometimes a schedule can be worked out for elementary school students. The teacher helps the child retrieve materials at the end of the school day for the first week, provides a direct reminder to the child during the second week, and gives a special signal such as a smile during the third week.

If an elementary school student has attended two full weeks of study periods or a high school student has sat through a full month of study periods without bringing home books and assignments, it is time to seek professional help to investigate the situation. Make arrangements for a psychological evaluation that includes educational testing to obtain a clearer definition of the problem.

Delays in Studying

Observe how long it takes your child to actually open a book and start working, noting the number of minutes under "Day." If a child begins working almost immediately, write a plus. If he spends more than two minutes looking around the room, shuffling papers, or winking at his sister, write a minus. Problems in this area can reflect rebelliousness, poor organizational skills, or difficulties settling in on a new task. Strive to appear busy and involved in your own work, thereby modeling proper behavior for a study period.

■ **Typical Problems.** To formulate a hypothesis about the reason for the child's delay, ask yourself the following questions. Record your observations in the "Comments" column.

★ Does the child look angry and defiant, with a "I'm not going to study and you can't make me" expression on his face? If so, rebelliousness may be the problem. Parents who do not try to control their child's actions, thus making it clear that it is indeed the child's choice to study, eliminate the need to rebel.

★ Is the youngster shuffling in random fashion through stacks of messy papers? If so, organization may be a problem for him. Ideas for helping children organize their materials are presented in the next chapter.

★ Are the papers neat and tidy, but he's squirming and having difficulty focusing his attention? This may be caused by the anxiety many people experience when making the transition from one activity to another. They are labeled procrastinators if they cope with anxiety by delaying. Children who are very anxious about new tasks may continue the first activity longer than is productive, rather than switching to the new one. Since tasks that are perceived as difficult produce more anxiety, children who anticipate the work will be hard may take longer to get started. Parents often mistakenly interpret such delays as a sign of rebelliousness. Expressing these worries helps reduce such anxieties. Ask whether the child has a lot of work to do; provide a sympathetic response or a few words of encouragement to help the child feel emotionally supported.

★ Does the child stare helplessly at his books, appearing anxious, overwhelmed, or afraid? Children who feel overwhelmed by the prospect of long and difficult assignments may benefit from being taught to organize their studies by breaking them down into small tasks. Parents may spend a few minutes before setting the timer to teach the child to outline and organize his studies. Ways to teach organization are discussed in the next chapter.

Interruptions Caused by the Studier

Parents often feel irritated when children interrupt their own study sessions, since the goal of getting them established on the program begins to feel like a fruitless fantasy. If the parent is in a bad mood to begin with, such interruptions can be most upsetting and many parents are tempted to criticize or scold to vent their frustrations.

Tallying interruptions caused by the studier and noting them under the "Comments" column gives parents something constructive to do. Remember that criticizing and scolding add more interruptions to the study period and give the child something concrete to struggle against. *Children who interrupt to express anger over having to study soon stop, if the parent remains silent while continuing to add time onto the study period.*

Tallying interruptions and taking notes also provides an objective framework for assessing the situation. It is easy to assume that a child who continually interrupts his session is being rebellious, but that is not necessarily the case. A parent who is angry may project anger onto the child, seeing her own feelings reflected in the child. When two or more children are on the program, filling in this journal section enables parents to see "which child is which." Otherwise, parents may feel as though no one is accomplishing anything given the large number of interruptions, when, in fact, one child may be getting a lot done, and the other is creating 90 percent of the interruptions.

■ **Typical Problems.** Many parents conclude their child is obstinate when he continues to interrupt his study periods. "When will he get it through his head that if he keeps interrupting his study period to get his materials, he has a longer study period?" they ask. While it is true that many children spend some time testing the limits, parents tend to attribute "bad" motivations to troublesome behaviors. It is easy to forget that everyone responds differently and possesses different skills and abilities. If parents have had a hard time consistently enforcing rules in the past, it may take a while for children to grasp that these limits will be enforced each time an interruption occurs. Children may feel confident they can get their parents to back down.

Completing this journal section also helps isolate problems with planning ability, distractibility, anxiety, or impulsivity. Determining whether interruptions should be rated plus for "not a problem" or minus for "a problem" is a subjective call. If your child concentrated for quite some time and interrupted to go to the bathroom, you may decide this does not reflect a problem and score it a plus. On the other hand, you may decide the child's frequent need to use the bathroom is a manipulation, and score it a minus indicating a possible problem.

Sometimes children are happy to have their study session last all evening, because they retain the parent's exclusive attention. Providing reinforcement in the form of additional time and attention outside of study sessions usually solves this problem.

Outside Interruptions

For this journal item, note events like "telephone call," "father came home," "brother turned on television," "baby cried," "sister walked into the kitchen." Write how many times a particular interruption occurs in a single study period. Evaluate each interruption by writing a plus sign if you think it was unavoidable and it was reasonable for the studier to react by looking up, talking, or getting up from the study table. If sister comes home from school, interrupts the studier to say "hello," and he pauses to return her greeting, you may decide this is not a problem.

Remember that not all interruptions are bad! The first few times you extend a study period due to an unavoidable interruption, remind the studier that the extra time is not a punishment. Say, "I have no objections to your stopping to spend a few minutes to say hello to your sister when she comes home, and hope you will continue to do this. I am extending your study period to make sure you still get your full time. Studying and greeting your sister are both important!" Studiers soon learn to ask their siblings not to bother them, work hard to ignore distractions, and remain focused on their work if they are anxious to finish their study period on time. Of course, if the parent determines that repeated interruptions are in violation of quiet time rules, they may need to take action to control the sibling.

Once studiers understand that their study periods are extended whenever their concentration is broken, most pretend not to be interrupted. They keep their attention tightly focused on their work in hopes of communicating, "See, I'm not being interrupted! I'm still studying!" It may be hard for parents to determine whether or not the studier was in fact interrupted, so I recommend they not add time if the child is trying to appear busy. This is the first step toward learning to screen out irrelevant stimuli altogether and requires considerable self-control.

Below is a list of common interruptions that occur during study periods. I have included some ideas for actions parents may take to try to control them.

■ **Infants.** When a baby needs attention, it usually requires an immediate response. Holding study periods at a time when a spouse is available to baby-sit may be the simplest solution in two-parent households. Paying older siblings to baby-sit may be an option in an emergency, but it is unreasonable to expect siblings to assume parenting responsibilities on a daily basis. Hiring another teenager to come to the house to baby-sit for the first few weeks may be a solution, if the family budget permits. Otherwise, the supervising parent should bring the baby to the study period, spread out a blanket on the floor, have supplies close at hand, and handle as much of the care (feeding, changing diapers) as possible in the study room.

■ **Toddlers.** Toddlers pose the greatest challenge to the supervising parent. Whenever possible, hold the study period after little ones are in bed. Otherwise, if parents bring an assortment of puzzles, books, crayons, blocks, and other toys to the study room and suggest the youngster play on the floor near the study table, it may help cut down on noise and movement. It is fine for little ones to move about the house and come and go from the study area. Encourage them to do so quietly, to whisper when addressing you, and to refrain from talking to studiers altogether by saying, "Shhh, you must not talk while your brother is busy studying." Toddlers will interfere with studying, however, and the goal should be to minimize the tendency for studiers to be distracted, rather than expecting study periods to be free of interruptions. Whenever the supervising parent must leave the room to check on toddlers, a brief apology should be extended to the studier for the interruption. The studier should also be allowed to take a break, and time should be added to the study period on the parent's return. When the parent is confident that work continues during her absence, there will be no need to compensate the studier for lost time.

■ **Other siblings.** Children age 5 and older who require constant parental attention either because they are too noisy or are misbehaving may be required to remain at the study table for the entire session. Be sure they have something to read or a project to work on. Say, "I'm sorry, but these continued interruptions are unfair to both your brother and me. I must extend his study period each time I have to stop to remind you to be quiet. This means your quiet time gets extended, too."

If the same problems occur the next day, the parent may require siblings to attend study periods for two days to help them remember. Remind siblings that they are welcome to join in at the study table at any time. This is particularly important since it is common for children to make noise or argue to get attention from parents. Even those who tease studiers about having to attend study periods may experience some jealousy over the amount of time and attention being dedicated to their sibling. Repeatedly inviting other children to join the study sessions is a way of offering a more productive method for getting attention.

■ **Adult household members.** It is sad but true that some husbands and wives have a hard time working together to protect the best interests of their children. When a controversy exists, the issue can often be traced to differing beliefs about what is truly best for the child. This controversy can usually be resolved through negotiating. The parent wishing to implement this program can suggest the spouse read this book before rendering judgement about its merits. If the spouse refuses to read about the program, or reads it but does not believe it is appropriate, the reasonable course of action is to discuss alternatives and develop a program both can support. Failing that, the parent should ask for support in implementing the program for a one-month trial. If the spouse is unwilling to assist by taking turns at supervising or helping with other children, try to obtain a commitment to respect the child's study period by observing quiet time.

Sometimes other adults are unable to observe quiet time. A senile live-in relative may continually wander into the study area and talk. An alcoholic spouse may insist on blasting the television throughout the child's study period, demanding as much attention from the supervisor as a toddler. The supervising parent may feel a tug of loyalties: Do I put my child's welfare above that of my spouse or mother? My answer is a definite "yes," but this is a decision each person must make.

If you are unable to get others to observe quiet time and cannot oust offenders from the house, the alternative is to find another location for the study periods. Libraries are wonderful, if they are accessible. Your office space or a neighbor's home may provide an option. Otherwise, a restaurant or diner can work fairly well. For the price of one soda per customer and a generous tip, most waiters and waitresses are happy to have you and your children spend time in their establishment each evening, before or after the dinner rush.

■ **Friends and relatives.** Telephone callers should be instructed to call back later, if the conversation interferes with the study period. Since all calls for studiers and the supervising parent cause an interruption, they aren't to talk on the telephone during study periods. Other family members may use the phone if conversations can be carried on in another part of the house. Visitors who drop by can be asked to come back after the study period.

■ **Televisions and stereos.** Not all students are distracted by noise from radio, television, and stereos. Some claim it enhances their concentration by helping them screen out other noise. I advise parents to disallow television and music in the study room, and to observe studier's reactions to determine whether music and sound tracks wafting in from other rooms create a distraction. Certainly there is no point in making a fuss about something that isn't bothering anyone. On the other hand, it is important for students to learn to study and concentrate without the white noise music provides, since radios are rarely allowed in classrooms.

The more noise a person can tolerate without becoming distracted, the better. Classrooms are never totally silent. Children fidget and whisper. The teacher walks around. Sounds from school hallways filter in. Work environments are noisy, too. Employees must concentrate despite the roar of machinery, ringing telephones, and conversations. The more easily distracted your child is, the more he needs to learn to ignore irrelevant stimuli. Provide a noise-free, movement-free environment to facilitate studying. The long-range goal is for the student to learn to stay on task regardless of environmental stimuli. A child will not learn to control his reaction to the environment, if the environment is always controlled for him.

End of Study Period

Under "Grade," write a plus if the study period ended on time, a minus if it ended late. Under "Comments" tell how many minutes the study period ran over schedule. The goal is to complete the study period close to the scheduled time.

Usually children have longer study periods during the first week and shorter ones after that. After the sixth day, siblings are better about observing quiet time, parents have developed methods for keeping toddlers and pre-schoolers entertained, and studiers begin bringing assignments home and only interrupt the session for legitimate reasons. As mentioned previously, an alternate pattern is for studiers to be very cooperative for the first week and then begin to test limits as the novelty wears off.

Voluntary Study

Surprise! Some of your children may voluntarily study beyond the required time. Note the length of time they continue to study in the column labeled "Day." Evaluating this item may not be very reliable if the youngster goes to his room to study or the supervisor leaves to do other things, so you may skip the evaluation and merely write a comment instead. In general, assign a plus if you feel your child's continued studying is a positive sign or a minus if you think it is a sign of trouble. It would be positive if a child who has shown little motivation in the past continues to study after the study period is over, if he missed school and is trying to catch up, or if he states he is working ahead. You might consider it a negative sign if your child tends to be compulsive or a perfectionist, or if he has put off a major project for a long time and is struggling to catch up. If the teachers seem to be assigning too much homework, this may also be a problem. Recommendations for handling these problems are discussed in chapters 7 and 8.

Helping Breaks

If you have scheduled breaks to answer questions, tutor, teach, or help with homework and studying, note how long you spend helping each studier. Evaluate the interaction writing plus if it seemed to go well and minus if you or your child experienced some discomfort. Explain in the "Comments" column what you believe caused the plus or minus. If a child asks you to test him on vocabulary words, you are happy to comply, and things go smoothly, give a grade of plus and write "quizzed on vocabulary." If things do not go well when you help, try to determine what caused the problem. Write, "I got frustrated when he made errors." "He was too critical of himself." "He claimed I was giving the wrong definitions." Use feedback from this section to determine the kinds of help and methods of helping that are most productive.

■ **Typical Problems.** Problems most often arise when parents or children lose patience. This can stem from feeling tired or irritable because of unrelated factors (it is late in the day, the parent or child is upset about other issues) or because problems arise as the parent and child interact.

Feelings of inadequacy about being able to explain or grasp the material frequently underlie problematic tutoring sessions. The child's difficulty verbalizing his thoughts or formulating questions may cause him to feel inadequate and may cause parents to become impatient. A parent's difficulty pinpointing the child's problem or being able to help may cause parents to feel inadequate and the child to become impatient.

It is important for parents to remember that when a parent teaches school lessons, a child learns much more than the particular material involved. He also learns:

★ "I am intelligent/not intelligent."

★ "I ask dumb questions/it is all right to ask questions."

★ "If my parent can't help me, no one can/there are other sources of information besides my parent."

★ "My parent has confidence I can learn this/my parent doubts I can learn this."

★ "Something is wrong with me for not catching on quickly/some things take a while to learn."

★ "I am bad for needing this kind of help./It's O.K. to need extra help."

It is important to remain aware of what both you and your child are feeling and stop helping as soon as either one of you is even a little upset. Leave the study table for a moment or two and suggest your child do the same. Getting away for a few moments often enables parents to get a clearer perspective on what was happening. If you are able to locate the source of the difficulty and think you can continue to help without becoming upset or upsetting your child, continue when you return. If not, help your child think of other ways to get answers to his questions. Often this will involve teaching the child to take the initiative to obtain extra help from a teacher or classmates. Methods for teaching this are discussed in chapter 7.

Parental Self-Evaluation

Tally the number of times you struggled with your studier. Note in the journal a plus if you refrained from struggling, a minus if you lost control. Ask your child for feedback to improve the accuracy of your impressions. Say, "Did I do or say anything that made you feel bad, hurt, or angry during this study period?" Under "Comments", write a brief plan noting how you might respond in the future should the same situation arise again. For instance, one parent who queried her children learned they were upset by the parent's response to friends that rang the doorbell. They agreed that in the future a studier would go to the door to greet visitors and ask them to come back later.

The daily journal is called the *Parent's Progress Journal* rather than the *Student's Progress Journal* for a reason. Keeping daily records enables you to assess your own progress in setting kind, firm, consistent limits. You will have succeeded when you set up the conditions whereby your child has a chance to study. The rest is up to the youngster.

If at the end of a month you are still having problems beginning and holding study periods, avoiding arguments and power struggles or enforcing limits, try to locate someone else to supervise the sessions. Seek counseling for yourself before again supervising daily study periods. If at the end of a month your child is still avoiding study periods, leaving books and assignments at school, or not using study periods to do homework, seek professional help for your child.

Phasing Out the Study Program

The final goal of this program is to get children to do their homework and study independently, without adult supervision. Once the parent has conducted regular study periods and the child has used the time productively for ten study sessions in a row, the parent may begin to gradually decrease supervision. This should be done in a controlled manner. Suddenly removing too much structure may create a setback. In taking small steps, the student can gradually adjust to increased autonomy.

Announce at the beginning of a session that you would like the studier to continue working a few minutes during your absence. After the studier has begun working, get up from the study table, leave the room for a few minutes, and notice whether he is still working when you return. If he seems to be, plan to leave twice the next day, three times the day after that, until you can come and go as needed.

■ **Typical Problems.** If your child appears to be distracted from his work when you return, remind him after the session has ended that he is to try to concentrate in your absence. Don't become angry! Remember that in misbehaving during a parent's absence the child may be saying any one of the following:

"I study because I care about pleasing you, not because I want what is best for me."

Parents in this situation may need to resign themselves to remaining with the child during study periods until he comes to value studying rather than merely complying with parental demands. Methods for helping instill this value are discussed in the next chapter.

"I don't know how to control myself when you're not here to control me."

This often occurs among children who are overdisciplined or overcontrolled. As soon as the parent is gone, they "run wild." Reconsider your overall approach to dealing with your child, and try to provide opportunities for increased autonomy. Allow more choices in other areas while helping him verbalize his angry feelings until his urge to act out when freed of parental constraints has diminished. This can take considerable time if the problems are severe. Obtaining individual or family counseling can help speed up the process. Otherwise, parents should plan to continue to supervise, while gradually allowing increased opportunities for autonomous functioning in other ways, until the child can control himself without a parent present.

"I like the attention or support I receive when you stay in the room with me."

Children who are very dependent or who do not receive enough attention may enjoy the closeness of having a parent with them when they study. Try to provide additional time together outside of study sessions and help your child function more independently following the methods outlined in the next chapter. In the meantime, rather than actually leaving the room, see if your child can tolerate your getting up and doing work away from the study table while remaining in the room.

Even though a child appears to be concentrating on his work when you return from a brief absence, it may be that he was distracted during your absence and pretended to be busy when he heard you approach. The best indicator of what transpires during your absences is changes in school grades. If the quantity and quality of homework deteriorates, it is safe to assume he is having a hard time coping with the increased independence. Obtain weekly reports from teachers using the Teacher's Feedback Form in the Appendix. Resume supervising sessions for at least a week, if school performance is suffering.

Continue to solicit feedback from teachers on a weekly basis for two more months. If a setback occurs, talk to your child using the problem-solving skills from the next chapter. Don't blame your child if problems recur! Such problems may mean you have misjudged your child's readiness for increased autonomy and need to spend more time at the study table.

Once your child has remained in charge of his own studies for two months and feedback from teachers has remained positive, consider your child out of the woods. Tell your studier you now believe he is capable of setting his own study schedule and choosing where he wants to study. Ask him to write out a schedule for himself. Allow him to choose times when no adult is available to supervise, but be sure he understands he is to follow the schedule he develops for five days, changing it only by submitting a request one day in advance. Reassure your child that if he is unable to follow his own schedule or the school reports a deterioration in his performance, you will reinstate the previous schedule so you can be home to help supervise.

Once he has planned his own schedule and teachers have continued to provide positive feedback for five days, celebrate! Cook his favorite meal, go on a special outing, or use another reinforcer. During the celebration announce that you believe he is now ready to make all his own decisions about when, where and how long to study.

Smoothing Out the Rough Spots

When children return to school from long holidays such as Thanksgiving, Christmas, and spring break, they often need additional structure for two or three days to help them settle in. Holidays which are particularly exciting, such as Halloween and Valentine's Day, may also cause a setback for elementary school children, although there is no vacation from school. Plan to reinstate regularly scheduled study periods at such times. Say, "This is such an exciting time of year, most children have a hard time concentrating on school work. For two days I want to be with you when you study. Tomorrow we will do it from 7:00 to 7:30; the next day from 8:15 to 8:45."

The hardest adjustment for children occurs following summer vacation, and I advise parents to reinstate the full program for at least two weeks at the start of every school year to help children settle in and make sure they get off to a good start. This is especially important if starting the new school year promises to be particularly stressful, such as at the beginning of middle school or high school.

Reinstating the program at the start of a new school year requires the creation of a new study schedule, which children appreciate since it gives them a clearer idea of how their days will be organized during the school year. Be prepared to make sudden changes in the schedule as other activities such as little league practices and choir rehearsals are announced.

Anticipate problem times and reinstate study periods before problems recur. Some children have a hard time at specific points during the academic year. Their scholastic performance deteriorates following predictable patterns. Some students begin each school year filled with a resolve to do better. They make a serious effort to study the first month, and slack off around the first of October. Other children consistently have a hard time around the holidays. Many show problems toward the end of the school year. Often it is impossible to determine the reason. Is the child ambivalent about moving on to the next grade? Is he overwhelmed by exams? Is he anxious about spending the summer with a relative, who lives far away? Parents need not know the why's and wherefore's to intervene.

The increased structure provided by the study program cannot hurt. It can only help. Anticipating difficulties and taking steps to protect a child is an important parental responsibility.

The study period may be reinstated to help your child cope with other problems. Is your child showing signs of depression or anxiety following a traumatic event? Begin holding supervised study periods until the crisis is past. Is a major change occurring in your household, such as an unemployed parent returning to work, the birth of a sibling, a move to a new neighborhood, a remarriage? Hold supervised study periods until the child has adjusted to the new situation.

Chapter 7

Best Ways to
Help with
Homework

Methods for helping children with homework may be divided into two categories: direct and indirect. When providing direct help, parents strive to accomplish a short-term objective such as helping a child complete a particular assignment or project, learn a school lesson, or prepare for a quiz or test. Indirect help focuses on enabling students to develop the behaviors, attitudes, and values so they can accept responsibility for homework and work independently. Methods of providing direct help include:

★ Reading and explaining directions in response to questions such as, "I don't understand what I'm supposed to do."

★ Answering informational or methodological questions such as, "What is the capital of Italy? How should I begin my essay?"

★ Providing feedback regarding the quality of work, including the checking of homework papers for accuracy, content, neatness, and spelling.

★ Teaching subject matter, as when parents explain how to solve trigonometry problems, conjugate irregular verbs, or look up words in a dictionary.

★ Giving answers, writing papers, or doing parts of projects, as in solving and providing answers to problems, dictating essays, or collecting fossils for a science project.

Although parents may accomplish a short-term objective by providing direct help, there are a number of dangers in doing so. Parents must ensure that their attempts to accomplish a short-term objective such as teaching academic material or helping a child complete a school assignment does not exacerbate other problems.

Building Self-Confidence

On one level, every time parents provide direct assistance they are also supporting the notion that the child cannot do the work on his own. This implication may undermine the child's self-confidence. Children who lack self-esteem are especially at risk for interpreting parental help as proof that they are incapable of doing the work.

To avoid this, parents need to provide concrete acknowledgement and positive reinforcement for each of the child's attempts and successes, no matter how small. Specifically, say such things as:

★ "Yes, it sounds like you were able to read and understand the instructions."

★ "It sounds like you were able to figure out exactly what you need to know, and stated your question very clearly."

★ "It looks like you understand the basic concept. Usually that's the hardest part. Let's look at your calculations."

★ "So you were able to read and understand the story on your own. It seems like you're uncertain about writing the summary."

★ "You read and followed the directions. You answered the first three questions correctly. Let's look at question 4."

★ "You understood the assignment. You chose a topic all by yourself. You came up with a creative idea."

★ "You understood how to work the problem after I gave only one example."

It is particularly important to provide feedback to help children accurately assess who is doing what. Otherwise, youngsters with poor self-esteem may perceive their parent as doing most or even all of the work, even if the parent's contribution is minimal.

After the parent has finished helping, the youngster should be asked to list all the things he did to solve the problems or learn the material. If the youngster is still not aware of having done anything, the parent should again list the child's accomplishments and be even more careful to point out the child's contributions when helping in the future.

Supporting Teachers

By providing direct help, parents may cast doubts on the teacher's competence. Unless the teacher has specifically delegated teaching or tutoring responsibilities to parents by asking them to help, children may interpret a parental decision to intervene as a way of saying, "Since the teachers aren't doing their jobs, I must do it for them."

When parents inquire about what happens at school (given that the child seems to lack the wherewithal to complete assignments), they provide an opportunity for children to denigrate teachers. Indeed, it is a rare child who responds, "Oh, I was talking to my friends instead of paying attention to the lecture, so my teacher wouldn't re-explain the material and answer my questions." More often the child's response leads parents to question the teacher's competence. Yet, there are undoubtedly many more inattentive students than there are poor teachers.

The potential for undermining teacher authority also arises when parents begin to help and suddenly the youngster proclaims, "You're doing it wrong," or "Our teacher told us..." By directly contradicting the teacher, parents may undermine the youngster's view of the teacher as a credible source. Telling the child he must have misunderstood causes some youngsters to become defensive and to struggle. Instead, strive for a tactful response which simultaneously encourages the student to think, question, investigate more thoroughly, and arrive at his own conclusions.

Supporting the Educational Process

Parental intervention may actually undermine the educational process. I know of one first year teacher who placed unrealistic homework demands on her students. So many parents were doing their children's homework, she had no idea her expectations were inappropriate. A parent who tried to discuss the problem with the teacher was told, "The other students manage." The complainant said no more. It wasn't until several parents shared their plight at a PTA meeting that they scheduled a meeting to talk to the teacher.

Although this is an extreme example, frequently students do not learn the material in school because of inadequate teaching. Many receive homework assignments which are poorly designed or inappropriate. Directions on worksheets may be confusing or poorly explained. In school districts where most parents are conscientious about helping their children at home, they may perpetuate these problems by depriving teachers of the feedback necessary to improve.

Writing notes to the teacher describing exactly what help you provided and encouraging other parents to do the same can alert the teacher to problems students are having mastering lessons or completing assignments.

Providing Feedback About Learning Problems

When parents provide direct help, they also risk undermining their child's education in significant ways. The quality of a student's homework and test results provides teachers with feedback regarding their success at teaching individual students and providing appropriate and meaningful assignments. When parents teach or help, they diminish the teachers' ability to assess whether their efforts are effective.

Many parents provide vast amounts of help with homework and teach many school lessons for years. When their children reach a level where the parent's own grasp of the material precludes giving much help, many students flounder. Parents who have their children evaluated are often shocked when previously undiscovered problems such as learning disabilities are pinpointed. They may feel angry with the school system that failed to uncover the problems years earlier, when in fact their own intervention prevented the student's problems from coming to the attention of school personnel.

Another adverse consequence of providing direct help at home is that parents lessen the need for children to pay attention in school. This is a particular problem during middle school years when students' social interests increase. If students can turn to parents to help them learn material they missed during the school day, they don't have to pay attention in class.

Promoting Assertiveness Among Students

Children who can count on parents to help them at home need not ask questions at school. Many students, particularly those who are shy, find it easier to solicit help from parents than from teachers and classmates. When parents ask why they don't request help at school, children often state that the teacher gets angry, refuses to answer questions, and does not let them ask classmates for help. Often these children are reacting to the fact that many teachers express irritation when students who don't pay attention ask for individual explanations. Sensitive children who are anxious to please may not realize teachers are willing to answer questions and provide extra help to those who pay attention and take school seriously. When parents answer questions students were too afraid to ask at school, children need not overcome their fears nor learn to assert themselves.

Parents need to discuss this problem with the teacher in an effort to determine whether the child's fears are realistic or groundless. Some teachers do get upset when students ask questions at inappropriate times. It is important for the child to be present so he may hear firsthand that he is welcome to ask questions or the teacher's reasons for not wanting to provide individual attention.

Promoting Independent Work

When parents provide direct help, they reinforce their child's dependency. Limiting assistance to scheduled breaks ensures the child will attempt homework on his own, before receiving help. Although a studier may appear to "just sit" during his study period and put off homework until he receives help during a scheduled break, most youngsters benefit from this quiet time. It reinforces their need to work alone.

If parents offer to provide help during scheduled breaks, children soon realize that help will be forthcoming. At that point, they become less anxious about being abandoned. Most then summon the courage to attempt some of the assignments on their own. In the meantime, parents should not insist they do the work themselves to avoid power struggles. Instead, they may simply suggest the studier spend the time looking over the material to organize questions.

Very dependent children may need breaks every few minutes, when first placed on the study program. Parents should provide the opportunity for the child to ask questions whenever a scheduled break arrives, even if the child is working! If the child has no questions, the parent can praise him. If the child suddenly invents questions, the parent should be careful not to lose patience. Remember that such questions may be a child's way of saying, "If I do my work by myself, can I still count on you to be here for me?"

To help a child take additional steps toward independence, parents should begin to lengthen the time between helping breaks. This should be done very gradually so as not to overwhelm the child. The next step for a youngster who has been allowed to ask questions every five minutes is to provide breaks for questions every six minutes.

Parents should also encourage children to seek help from other sources including classmates, siblings, and older neighborhood children. Once a student can comfortably turn to other individuals and resource materials, he is functioning independently.

Promoting Student Responsibility

Children who ask for help are demonstrating a responsible attitude since they are attempting to see that their work gets done. However, many ask questions to involve parents in homework, and then proceed to relax while the parents do much of the work.

Parents must carefully assess each request for help and limit the amount of assistance. In the event a parent feels manipulated or decides he is doing too much, he should avoid responding critically, turn the work back over to the child, and exercise greater caution the next time a request for help is forthcoming.

When parents provide direct help, lines of responsibility become blurred. No longer is it the teacher's responsibility to teach and evaluate the student's work and the student's responsibility to learn, do homework, and study. Many parents who complain about the irresponsibility of teachers and students contribute to it by assuming much of the responsibility themselves. Although the parents' motivation is to help, their focus on short-term solutions may perpetuate other problems. Teachers and students need not be responsible as long as someone else assumes their responsibilities for them!

Providing help only during structured breaks can be a first step toward clarifying lines of responsibility. It can be the parent's way of saying, "I am responsible for helping you at specific times; otherwise, you are responsible for your own work."

Promoting Positive Attitudes Toward Learning

Few parents have the expertise to teach all subjects to their youngsters. More importantly, relationships between parents and children are so intense that they usually lack the objectivity needed to teach effectively. That is why we have public education and professional teachers.

Parents often feel inadequate when trying to decipher material in textbooks and homework instructions. Determining the source of a youngster's confusion and finding ways to explain concepts can be very difficult. Just as most parents panic at the prospect of toilet training a youngster ("What if he never learns?"), they panic when their child has a hard time learning ("Is he slow, lazy, or just not trying?" "What is wrong with me for not being able to get this information across?"). When people are panicked, they do not make good teachers. They cannot think clearly or modulate their responses to ensure they are acting in their own, much less someone else's, best interests.

Many children resent parental intrusion in any form. Some feel guilty obtaining help from parents since many teachers emphasize the importance of doing assignments independently. Students may feel they are cheating by not doing the work themselves. They ask for help but become upset when their parent complies. Power struggles ensue as parents attempt to respond to mixed messages. "Please show me how to do this," children ask one minute. "You're doing it wrong!" they may proclaim the next.

It is easy for parents to become frustrated in this situation. If possible, however, parents can guard the youngster's autonomy by saying, "Do you really think so?" Then, I highly recommend parents retreat, and provide encouragement by saying, "I'm glad you think you've got it figured out. Your teacher can let you know if there's a problem when she looks over the paper."

Learning by making mistakes has its own value. Further, it is the student's work, not the parent's, so it is important that the student remain in charge. Allow him the freedom to ask questions and then reject the answers. Homework is the child's turf. To push one's own opinions about how a problem should be solved can imply that it would be terrible for the youngster to make an error.

In the end, a child's attitude toward studying and learning are more important than any individual school lesson. Negative experiences continue to influence attitudes long after the "helping" has ended.

To promote positive attitudes:

★ Admit to your own inadequacies when communication is breaking down.

★ Seek alternative ways for your child to obtain help.

★ Never promote yourself as the only one who can lend assistance.

★ Do not become defensive if your child insists you are wrong; allow him to do it his way, and let the teacher make corrections.

★ Express confidence in your child's ability to figure things out himself, to reach out to classmates for help, and to ask the teacher for help.

★ Allow your child to remain in charge!

Providing Indirect Help

While direct help focuses on achieving short-term goals, indirect help enables children to achieve the long-term goals of accepting responsibility for their school work and functioning independently. To accomplish these objectives, parents must help children improve their skills at remembering, planning ahead, organizing their work, concentrating, persevering, taking initiative, problem-solving, and functioning autonomously. It also helps if parents provide positive reinforcement for studying. They must also allow children to experience failure, if necessary, rather than protecting them from what may sometimes be difficult realities.

Student Planners

The simplest tool for helping students remember is a basic assignment book. Expanding an assignment book into a specially designed planner solves a host of other study problems: It can assist the disorganized high school student who drifts through his days in a fog of confusion, a conscientious middle school student who worries about forgetting an important assignment or test, or a primary school child who is just learning how to manage homework. Given that children's lives are busier and their schedules more complex than in the past, it is an unusual student who will not find benefit from a planner. I consider students' need for one as basic as their need for pens and pencils. The sample page in the Appendix can be adapted to meet the needs of individual students in developing a suitable planner.

In addition to providing a central place to note assignments, upcoming tests, quizzes, and special homework instructions, be sure to include a separate space for listing supplies needed to do the work. Advise your youngster to list them at the time assignments are given. There should also be sufficient space for noting miscellaneous items that need to be brought home or returned to school the next day such as permission slips, gym clothes, or a report card.

It is important to include a column labeled "Time" in which students estimate how long each task will take. This time-management device helps students budget study periods. Providing a special space for determining an order for working on assignments encourages students to organize their study period to use their time effectively. Include a column for students to check off assignments as they complete each one. This simple strategy provides them with a sense of accomplishment by helping to focus on successes. It also makes it easier to tell at a glance which assignments were not completed, so they can be carried over onto the next day's sheet.

Long-range projects or tests scheduled for some time away should be listed each day until the due date. Describing which parts of the project are to be done or which material is to be reviewed on particular days helps children complete work without resorting to a last minute marathon session. Breaking large projects into smaller tasks also makes them seem less overwhelming.

Teaching Study Skills

Most children need in-depth help to master the skills needed to manage their studies responsibly. Parents can teach the skills described below during interactions with their children in all areas of their daily lives.

Teaching Students to Plan Ahead

To do homework effectively, children must be able to plan ahead. When an assignment is given, they must look it over and anticipate problems, and ask questions. Before leaving school, they must decide which books and materials they need for that evening. They must plan their evening schedule to allow adequate time for their studies.

Often children are reprimanded for failing to plan ahead, yet no one has spent time teaching them how. When life was less busy and parents had more time to interact with their children, youngsters learned the process of planning ahead by hearing their parents verbalize their thoughts prior to taking action.

Consider that in days gone by a mother was likely to say, "I'm going to fix spaghetti for dinner tonight, so I must defrost the hamburger. When I go to the grocery store, I must remember to pick up garlic." When they arrived home from school, children heard her talk as she continued to make preparations for the evening meal. "If I prepare the rolls and the noodles in ten minutes, they should be done about the same time." In other words, they heard her plan ahead.

Modern parents are likely to make their plans during the commute home from work while the child is at home or in day-care. From the child's perspective, the meal and many other household events just "happen." They don't hear about the planning that goes into day-to-day activities.

Parents need to verbalize their thoughts when planning something, be it a trip to the grocery store, paying bills, or going on a vacation, so that children have an opportunity to learn the process. *If your child has problems planning ahead, try to share your own plans for doing something at least once a day.* Include your children when you are making plans. Unless youngsters are frequently included in the planning of activities, they won't know what items to consider when making preparations.

Help children make plans of their own. Planning ahead requires learning to ask the right questions. As you discuss your own plans, the child learns the kinds of issues to consider and the kinds of questions to ask. Remember that scolding a child for failing to plan ahead does not teach him how to do things differently! If you feel irritated with a youngster who doesn't "stop to consider," channel your frustration into spending more time helping him learn how to do so.

Teaching Organizational Skills

When children are taught to pick up their toys, personal belongings, or bedroom, they learn the basic skills needed to organize their school materials. To help students overcome organizational problems, teach them to organize not only school papers but all their possessions.

Again, the first step is modeling. By keeping the house free from clutter and making sure belongings are neatly arranged, parents provide a daily example of how to organize. The second step is to guide children through the process by having them participate. Since to organize one must have a grasp of the underlying categories, parents must teach children the different ways objects may be sorted. If a child is simply directed to "clean up your room," he may randomly stuff all his belongings into drawers and closets without thinking about the advantages of designating certain spaces for particular items. Discuss ways to categorize items by providing ideas about how to sort them so they will be easier to find.

Similarly, if a child continually misplaces notes and worksheets, show him how to organize his school papers. Be sure to have him watch as you do this and explain each step. Say, "You have six folders (or six sections in this notebook), one for each of your five subjects and an extra one for miscellaneous papers such as permission slips, notes from your teacher, pages of doodles, notes from friends. First, write the name of each subject on a folder (or index tab). Write 'miscellaneous' on the last one. Next, let's put the papers in the folders. Is this a math paper? Then I will put it in this folder."

I have known parents who, on hearing about such organizational problems during a school conference, actually go to school and clean out their child's desk or locker. They go through every paper and notebook and create a filing system. A week later they discover chaos has returned and they become angry. *Many parents forget that doing something for a youngster and teaching him to do things for himself are very different. The first procedure encourages dependence; the second helps students become independent.* Don't expect organizational problems to be solved until you have taught your child how to do it!

Time Management for Students

Learning to budget time is another important study skill. If your child has deficits in this area, teachers probably have noted that he has problems "using time wisely." To teach a youngster to budget time, parents should verbalize their own plans. For instance, say, "I have three errands to run, and I must be home in an hour. The trip to pick up Jessica should take fifteen minutes, the stop at the dry cleaners should take five, and the trip to the grocery store should take thirty minutes. That will leave ten minutes extra, so even if traffic is heavy we should be home in time."

Students who don't know how to budget and allocate time may spend the entire study period working on a science paper that isn't due for a week, neglecting to prepare for a French test the next day. Parents need to teach these youngsters how to budget their study sessions.

To do this, have the child review each subject and estimate how long each activity will take to complete before beginning the study period. If the child doesn't know how to estimate the time, suggest he read the directions, look over each assignment, and take a guess.

In the event that there does not appear to be sufficient time to complete all the work, he will need to prioritize the assignments. Items which are due the next day usually need to be completed first. Projects which aren't due for several days may be put off. Compulsive studiers often need help dealing with the realities of time and making decisions about how best to utilize it until they learn to prioritize. Many students who procrastinate become discouraged, believing that since they can not complete everything, there is no point in doing anything at all.

If the length of the study period and the time needed to complete assignments coincide, students can then decide on the order. Ask whether the child prefers doing hard things first or easy things first. Some students like to do work on their favorite subjects first and save the ones they don't like until last. Still others prefer to get the "bad" jobs over with and save the best until last, like dessert. Help your child develop an order for doing assignments that is most pleasing to him.

If it appears that a child will be able to complete all the work and have time left over, parents should suggest working ahead, pointing out that they will already know some of the material their classmates are trying to learn. Many students, particularly those who do not do well in school, are enthusiastic about the prospect of surprising their friends and teachers by already knowing some of the material. In fact, I know a number of students, having long since resigned themselves to their position at the bottom of the class, who immediately overcame their discouragement and made it a habit to work ahead. They discovered this tactic enabled them to keep up or even excel in school.

Some students need help deciding how to structure long-range projects. Children who become overwhelmed at the prospect of major projects often do not know how to divide them into smaller tasks and create a schedule for working on specific aspects of a large assignment. Discuss the various steps to be completed and have your child estimate how long each will take, then enter the plan in his planner.

Since studying for a test or exam over several days is more effective than cramming during a single study session, parents also need to teach their children how to create a schedule to study for major tests. It is easy for people (including adults) to feel overwhelmed by the need to study for an exam that requires a review of an entire semester's material. Many attempt to assuage their discomfort by procrastinating or avoiding studying altogether. Help your child develop a plan. Reviewing two chapters per night for a week seems much less intimidating than tackling ten chapters.

Improving Concentration

Problems with distractibility afflict many students, making it difficult for them to concentrate. First and foremost, avoid making blanket statements which encourage your child to fulfill negative expectations. Saying, "he can't concentrate," or, "he's distractible," suggests the child has character traits or biological problems which are to blame.

To improve concentration children must first recognize when they are concentrating, so they can begin to recognize how they block out potentially distracting stimuli. When you see your youngster concentrating, be it on a T.V. show, book, or game with a friend, point it out! Often parents ignore these accomplishments. In stating, "he only concentrates when he wants to," they discount the fact that the child does possess the ability to concentrate. In so doing, they encourage the child to disregard his capability as well.

Notice events that cause your child to become distracted and provide verbal feedback, along with suggestions for improvement: "Perhaps you are having a hard time concentrating on this chore, because you are so anxious to go outside and play. If you could think instead about ways to do the job faster, perhaps you could finish sooner"; or "It may be that trying to build your model and watch T.V. at the same time makes it hard to concentrate. If you turned off the television or waited until your show ended to do the model, you might make fewer errors."

Since anxiety is a common cause of distractibility, providing opportunities for children to talk about their troubles helps immensely. Many people believe talking about troubles makes matters worse. Although the child may appear more upset when discussing problems, his subsequent concentration is likely to improve.

People have a hard time concentrating when they are not physically up to par. Provide verbal feedback to increase your child's awareness of this dynamic: "Maybe you are having a hard time concentrating because you are tired. Why not get a magazine and lie down on the couch to rest for a few minutes?" In time, children learn to assess the factors that are interfering with concentration and also learn how to rectify the situation.

Encouraging Perseverance

Students who have difficulties persevering usually have a low tolerance for frustration. They become upset when they perceive tasks as difficult, and resolve their discomfort by switching to another activity. To help your child, the first step is to tune into his feelings: Note when he is becoming tense and help him talk about it. Say, "You look like you're getting frustrated. Does this work seem hard?"

Children with poor tolerance for frustration almost always suffer from feelings of insecurity. Their lack of self-confidence about their ability to do the assigned task causes them to give up. Further, they place pressure on themselves to perform, and then become upset if their work is less than perfect. The harder they try, the harder it is for them to think clearly; the quality of their efforts declines as frustration mounts. Frustrated children may throw away or tear up their homework papers. Parents may think they don't care when they fail to complete or turn in assignments. In truth, the problem is they care too much. They would rather turn in nothing than turn in work they judge to be substandard.

Hearing adults recount times when they experienced similar self-doubts and frustrations is especially soothing and reassuring to children and helps build their self-confidence: "Sometimes at work when I'm typing and I make a mistake, I feel like I'm a failure and I get upset with myself, too. But I know that everyone makes mistakes sometimes; that's just the way it is. None of us is perfect."

Some children have a hard time persevering on tasks they find tedious or boring. Their frustration stems from their anger over being required to do work which does not hold their interest. Helping them find creative ways to complete routine assignments can sometimes help. Providing emotional support by sympathizing with their plight helps many persevere despite waning motivation. (Teachers should be notified if the student is underchallenged to see if more stimulating work can be assigned.)

Encouraging Initiative

There are many books available that teach parents how to create richer educational environments at home. Read them and follow their advice! Students are more likely to be interested in learning and take initiative with their studies, if their family not only values education but incorporates educational activities on a day-to-day basis at home. Having opportunities to apply school learning to every day life does wonders for motivating students.

First, parents must know what material is being covered at school. Instead of posing general questions like, "What did you learn in school today?" ask more specific ones, such as "What are you studying in English?" "What types of poems are you reading?"

Next, be creative in developing real-life experiences that support and expand upon school subjects. Is your youngster uninterested in learning about fractions? Have him help you bake half a cake; let him be the one to cut the pie or jello into fifths. Is it hard to get him to read? See if you can find a magazine on a subject of interest to subscribe to. Does he need to practice writing? See if he would like to have a pen pal. Is he studying Spanish? Take him to see a foreign film, to eat in a foreign restaurant, and point out Spanish phrases you come across. Is his class learning about the Civil War? Plan a family outing to a museum containing relics from that era.

Identify your youngster's natural interests and encourage him to learn more about them by sharing what you know about the subject. Ask your child to teach you about things he is learning at school that interest you. This provides tremendous incentive for students to pay closer attention and put greater effort into academics. Talk to your child. Find as many ways to apply what he is learning in school to his everyday life.

Solving Homework Problems

The techniques executives use to resolve business problems work very well in solving homework problems. Parents can teach children to use problem-solving methods to resolve school and homework difficulties by guiding them through the steps.

■ **Identifying the problem.** The first step to solving a problem is to clearly identify it. "Johnny doesn't bring home his assignments." "Jane doesn't understand how to write an expository essay." "Jack is failing social studies." Examine each problem separately. Trying to solve several problems at the same time is confusing and causes parents and children alike to feel overwhelmed.

■ **Determining the cause of the problem.** Most parents and professionals have difficulty with this step. This is because the most reliable source of information is the child, and relationships between adults and children are such that adults often refrain from asking about the problems and children are reluctant to share what they know. The fear of being chastised or blamed makes them reticent about opening up, so provide reassurance that you want to help.

Often children do not know the cause of a problem and must be helped to identify it. Unless adults ask straightforward questions about sensitive issues, it may be impossible to pinpoint the source. Regardless of the particular type of homework or study problem a child is having, it is important to ask questions:

The subject. What are you studying in that course right now? Is it too hard? Is it too easy? Do you like what you're learning? Does it seem worth the trouble? What could the teacher do differently so you'd like learning this subject more or be more interested in it?

The teacher. How do you like your teacher? Is he nice or mean? Does he scare you or make you angry? Does he expect too much or not enough from students? Do you understand what he says? Do you feel interested or bored in his class? Does he get mad if students ask questions? What kind of rules does he have? Do the rules seem fair or unfair? What would he have to do differently for you to like him better?

The classroom. Can you see the board? Can you hear when the teacher talks? Are things too noisy? Too quiet? Is it hard to concentrate? Do you like where you sit? What could be different so you would like your classroom better?

Classmates. Is anyone bothering you? Giving you problems? Do you have any friends? Do you get teased? Are there any students you wish weren't in your class, or weren't in your school? Why? Are there any students you wish could be in your class? Why?

Tests and quizzes. What do you think about the tests and quizzes in this class? Are they too hard? Too easy? Too confusing? Do you understand the directions? Are the grades fair? Do you have too many tests or not enough?

The homework. Does the teacher explain what you're supposed to do? Do you always understand the directions? Does the teacher answer your questions? Is class time provided to work on it? Is the homework graded? Are the grades fair or unfair? Does it take too long to do the assignments? Are the assignments too hard? Too easy? Too boring?

Special projects. Does the teacher explain exactly what you are supposed to do? Does she give you enough time? Too long a time? Do you get to go to the library at school? Can you find the things you need in the library?

A word of caution: Most parents and even many professionals are reluctant to ask these kinds of questions. They fear that by even raising the possibility that the teacher is mean, has unfair rules, or doesn't explain things clearly, they may undermine the teacher's authority. Of course, children have their own opinions about such issues. In asking such questions, adults are merely encouraging the child to express his ideas, so the problems can be resolved. It is usually more dangerous not to ask than to ask difficult questions!

If you ask these questions and don't like the answers, it is important to keep your feelings to yourself! If a child says, "My teacher is mean because she makes us do math" and you respond by defending the teacher or criticizing the child, two things are likely to happen. First, the child won't tell the rest of the story. Second, he will be more reluctant to answer questions in the future.

Remember that what children say and what they mean may be very different. Sorting out their meanings requires an open mind and lots of listening. This is true of adolescents as well as of younger children. Statements that initially sound ridiculous, exaggerated, or far-fetched may sound quite differently when clarified. The child who said her fourth grade teacher was mean for making students do math went on to explain that the teacher required students to do papers in ink. She counted answers wrong if students crossed out numbers. On tests and quizzes, the rule was the same: Students could not cross out mistakes, could not erase anything, and were forbidden to use scratch paper. Had the child initially been criticized for calling the math teacher "mean," his reason for viewing her in this way might not have been revealed.

Brainstorming Solutions

Once the cause of the problem has been identified, the next step is to search for ideas. Brainstorming, which requires participants to list every idea that comes to mind, is the most effective method for developing ideas. When brainstorming, all proposals, no matter how outlandish, should be written down. Censoring suggestions inhibits children's participation and dampens the creativity of all participants.

Youngsters often become silly when encouraged to create ideas without concerning themselves as to whether or not they would actually work. It is common for their humorous solutions to contain some very good ideas. An added benefit of encouraging humor is that it relieves tension.

Select and Implement Proposed Solutions

After everyone runs out of ideas, the proposed solutions should be methodically evaluated, eliminated, or refined. In many cases, the participation or cooperation of a classroom teacher is needed to implement a solution. Sometimes other school personnel such as principals, counselors, or coaches need to be involved. Parents are often afraid to confront, ask for additional help, or seek special consideration from school personnel on behalf of their child, fearing the teacher's retaliation. However, a study of competent children found that those who were doing well in school had one thing in common: Their parent was in continual contact with school personnel, calling, writing, and going to school to advocate every time a problem arose. Do not hesitate to call upon teachers or other educators for help! Ask them to help brainstorm solutions to find one they believe will work.

Evaluating Results

Effective problem-solving requires that results be carefully evaluated. Sometimes solutions that sound great in theory fail to accomplish the desired objective. Also, there is a tendency for some problems to remain hidden until others have been solved. For instance, a student may have difficulty remembering to bring his physical science textbook home to do his homework, so he receives poor grades. Once this problem is solved and he brings the book home, the reading level may prove to be too advanced for him to comprehend.

■ **Problem-solving in action.** *The number one error parents and professionals make when talking to children is filling up the pauses rather than allowing adequate time for youngsters to respond.* Adolescents often need as much or more time than younger children to collect their thoughts. Remember that a youngster need not talk if the adult does all the talking for him! A student may seem particularly resistant to discussing homework, because he says very little. However, silence at the beginning of a discussion occurs because the child is uncomfortable; later it usually means the child is listening and thinking.

Functioning Autonomously

Despite the fact that a parent may be successful at getting her child's educational needs met, the final goal is for students to learn to speak up in their own behalf. Parents who know that their child can ask questions, solicit help, confront the teacher and classmates, and take charge to implement solutions can realize that their youngster has what it takes to function autonomously.

Many students are afraid to state their needs or assert themselves with teachers because the balance of power in the classroom places them in an inferior position. Further, few youngsters know how to confront a teacher appropriately. Parents need to support the development of autonomous behavior by handling most of the special contacts with teachers initially, then gradually turning over more responsibility to the child as he becomes more confident and competent. The child should be included whenever his parent contacts the teacher, be it by letter, phone, or in person, so he can begin to learn how such contacts are handled.

Since so many parents work, most contacts with teachers occur through letters and notes. Structure the letter-writing so the child assumes increasing responsibility for it.

First, the parent writes a letter with the child's input. The parent reads the final letter to the child, signs it, and the child takes the letter to school.

> *"Dear Mrs. Smith, Johnny is having trouble concentrating because a boy who sits nearby talks a lot. Would it be possible to change the seating arrangement? Sincerely, Mrs. Jones."*

Second, the parent writes a letter with the child's input, and they both sign it. In so doing, the child gains a sense of communicating with the teacher more directly. Although many students express fears that the teacher will be angry with them, having the parent's signature appear next to theirs provides reassurance that they are not facing the teacher alone.

> *"Dear Mrs. Smith, Johnny didn't do his grammar homework because he doesn't understand the difference between adjectives and adverbs. Could you explain this again? Sincerely, Mrs. Jones and Johnny."*

Third, the parent and child develop the letter, but the child writes the letter in his own handwriting and both he and the parent sign it.

> *"Dear Mrs. Smith, I lost my government textbook. How do I go about getting another one? Can I wait to take the test until I've had a chance to replace it and study? Sincerely, Johnny and Mrs. Jones."*

Fourth, the parent and child develop the letter together as before. However, the child writes it in his own handwriting, signs it, and takes it to school.

> *"Dear Mrs. Smith, Even though I make good grades on my homework and study long hours, I continue to make poor grades on the tests. Do you have any suggestions as to how to improve my grades in your class? Sincerely, Johnny."*

By this point, most students feel confident enough to ask questions and discuss problems directly with the teacher, and do not feel the need to write a note. If a student is having a hard time taking the next step and talking to the teacher in person, provide a similar structure to help the child overcome fears and learn these skills. To do this, you will need to accompany the child to school or have three-way telephone conversations.

First, the parent does most of the talking but provides openings for the child to talk. Second, the child does most of the talking, with the parent helping out if the child gets stuck, thereby serving as a mediator. Third, the child talks to the teacher by herself. If the student is dissatisfied with the results of the conversation, the parent offers to go to the school to assist.

Just as there is no way to teach a child to cross the street alone, until he reaches a certain level of competence, there is no way to teach a child to handle school problems himself, until he has developed self-confidence and know-how. Children are able to resolve school and homework problems, once they know how to assert themselves. I have seen the meek, timid children blossom after a single successful encounter.

Providing Reinforcement That Works

Many parents try to bargain or make deals with their children to get them to do homework. "I'll buy you a special present," they say. Or, "We'll have a picnic this weekend if you do your work each day for a week."

This method of providing positive reinforcement usually backfires. Presents and special privileges fail to keep students motivated, because there aren't realistic rewards which provide enough incentive.

Even the promise of a wonderful present, like a bicycle or stereo at the end of the semester, rarely works. It is hard for children, including adolescents, to remain motivated day in and day out, week in and week out, month in and month out, for a reward that is so far away. (Besides, a child who can tolerate waiting that long may be able to save up his own money or wait until his birthday to ask for his heart's desire!) *To be motivating, reinforcers must be immediate.*

When families negotiate rewards and students remain unmotivated, many parents become upset. "But you promised!" they say. "You said you'd study if I gave you that toy." Children just shrug their shoulders and don't say anything when confronted. A few point out the contract's escape clause: "That's O.K., I decided I don't want to watch T.V. tonight." This is a way of saying, "Go ahead and withhold the privilege, I won't do my homework, and we'll be even!" For presents and privileges to be effective, parents may need to renegotiate rewards every day.

Even when the reinforcers "work" and the child studies, parents often become disillusioned with the strategy. "As long as I keep to the agreement by taking him to the movies on the weekend, he does his homework. Otherwise, he does nothing at all. He should be doing his work for himself, not because he wants to see movies." Parents need to consider the long-range implications of providing reinforcers.

Real-Life Rewards

The best reinforcers are those that help make homework and studying pleasant. Having a parent and other siblings present at the study table helps make it a more social affair. Sharing afterwards about what everyone read and learned makes studying more meaningful and is reinforcing.

Helping children apply what they learned in school to every day life provides them with a reason and purpose for it all. This is particularly important for adolescents. "John, you're studying French. I have a colleague from Morocco. Can you teach me a few French expressions?" "Jane, you just did a report on Gandhi for social studies. In the Martin Luther King celebration, they mentioned Gandhi several times. Who was Gandhi, anyway? What did he do?" ""Jack, our family is in the 15 percent tax bracket. You're studying percentages. Can you help me calculate how much tax I owe?"

The Gift Of Time

The one reinforcer guaranteed to appeal to youngsters which parents can give without feeling guilty is time. *Plan to spend time playing or interacting with your child after his study periods whether or not he used the time productively, especially during the first two weeks.* This is yet another way to say, "I'm not requiring you to attend study periods to punish you."

Spending just fifteen pleasant minutes per evening to provide reinforcement for studying can make a tremendous difference. However, I recommend parents refrain from promising to do so. Rather, simply suggest a game or sit down next to a teenager shortly after the study period has ended, without specifying that you are offering time and attention as a reward. Children become increasingly willing to study if you spend pleasant time with them afterwards, even though you haven't told them why you have become so generous with your time!

Engaging in pleasant time together builds and solidifies parent/child relationships. The desire to please parents forms the basis of children's wishes to meet societal demands and expectations. Achieving the final goal of studying and doing homework out of concern for one's own well-being comes later. In the meantime, if your child won't do it for himself, be glad that he is doing it to please you!

Using Outside Sources To Provide Extra Help

If a student needs or wants more help than the teacher can provide, a tutor may be needed. Tutors have varied backgrounds, abilities, and fees.

They range in price from about $75 to zero per hour: Often you may barter their services to avoid having to pay in cash.

Professional tutors are the most expensive. Despite degrees and credentials, they don't necessarily provide the best help. The tutor's personality and ability to relate to the child are as important as academic training. To find a professional tutor, ask your school for recommendations. Inquire about the tutor's philosophy to learn if building self-confidence and promoting independent work are important goals. Ask for references. Talk to parents of children who have been helped in the past. To best utilize the tutor's talents, ask what specific educational enrichment activities you can do at home.

Older children may provide peer tutoring. Many high schools have peer tutoring programs, and you may be able to hire a teenager who is skilled and interested in earning extra money. Peer tutors are able to relate to students' difficulties mastering subject matter, since they learned the same material and were exposed to classmates grappling with the same problems, just a few years before.

Siblings, even those who have difficulties getting along, often do well when placed together in a tutoring situation. Younger ones are delighted to have the attention of an older brother or sister. Older ones may be delighted to give attention, especially if they are being paid for their efforts. In employing the services of an older sibling, develop a definite schedule with clear responsibilities and remuneration. Not all siblings can tolerate working together in this way, so attempting to have them do so is a gamble. If it doesn't work out, it should not be viewed as a failure on either youngster's part.

Academically-inclined elementary school children love to play school. Many have a natural gift for teaching others and make excellent tutors. If your child is having other adjustment problems, the tutoring sessions may help him cement a relationship with a desirable classmate as well, which may have a positive effect on your youngster's social adjustment. Do not hesitate to contact parents of some classmates, if you see this as a viable option. At the very least, the other parents will be flattered that you consider their child bright enough to serve in this capacity. If the classmate's parents work and you do not, sending their child to your home after school a few days a week may even solve some of their baby-sitting, day-care, or transportation problems.

Senior citizens who have the time, energy, and talent to provide academic help make excellent low-cost, high-quality tutors. Recent trends are to solicit senior volunteers to provide one-on-one tutoring during the school day in a number of districts.

Allowing A Child To "Fail"

The fear that a child may fail a homework assignment, a project, a quiz, a test, an exam, or a year in school is a big one for parents. This fear leads many to become overinvolved in homework, to accept too much responsibility for the child's work, and to panic when problems arise. Some parents in this situation become so desperate, they resort to artificially preventing failure.

★ They do portions of the child's work.

★ They engage in tutoring and teaching sessions so fraught with conflict that parent and child alike emerge feeling upset and angry.

★ They cover up irresponsible behavior by making up and signing written excuses to the teacher to obtain extensions, special considerations, or favors for the student.

★ They advise the child on ways to manipulate the teacher into granting extensions for late work.

★ They pressure teachers into passing the student or raising his grade for the semester or the year.

★ They refuse to allow the child to be retained in school even though he has not mastered the material at his current level.

So as not to discourage the youngsters (or because they cannot withstand pressures exerted by the parents), some teachers participate in the deception by giving students higher grades than they deserve. The long-range consequences for the student can be tragic. Like their counterparts in the business world, too many students are promoted to their level of incompetence until their deficiencies are exposed. At that point, the deficiencies may seem overwhelming, and the students give up and drop out.

Sometimes parents (and even teachers) justify rescuing a student by saying they believe he should be rewarded for having tried. They fear the youngster will become discouraged, if he receives the grade he deserves. The irony is that a potent way to help students is to allow them to fail, when they deserve it. Often, repeating a course or an entire year of school is the best way to encourage and motivate them.

A student's failure can be hard for a parent to accept. In fact, failing is usually harder on parents than on students. Parents who attempt to prevent a child from experiencing the consequences of poor scholastic performance need to carefully consider whose interests they are trying to serve. Parents who cannot cope with a child's failure usually have poor ego boundaries;

they personalize their youngster's failure and experience it as if it were their own.

Why is it dangerous to protect a child from failure?

First, consider what grades are all about. They are a mechanism for providing feedback to the student. A parent who prevents a student from receiving a low or failing grade distorts reality for the child, resulting in false feedback. The student derives a false sense of his strengths and weaknesses. Although avoiding confrontations with reality may help a child feel better in the short-run, it is guaranteed to create confusion in the long-run.

One of the brighter youngsters I worked with had no sense of her intelligence or competencies. Her father had always redone her assignments for her, dictated her essays, written her term papers, done her science projects, even bullied teachers into giving her higher report card grades than she deserved. In the process, the student had, in fact, learned her school lessons. Her achievement tests were above grade level in every subject. However, she didn't think she was bright at all. Otherwise, why would her parent cover for her? By ninth grade, she had lost all motivation. She saw no point to doing anything: Her father would redo it, anyway.

Comparing her work to her father's was a severe blow to her ego. He could always learn and do the material better and faster than she could. Lacking feedback from teachers (since the work was not her own), she had no basis for judging the quality of her personal progress or efforts. She could not sort out her own contributions to the final product of their combined efforts. Would she have gotten a B instead of an A if her father hadn't helped her, or maybe even an F? Over the years she had become convinced she was totally incompetent, and assumed her father was what stood between herself and certain failure. Her high achievement test scores meant as much to her as her grades: absolutely nothing. If her teachers could be fooled, why couldn't the tests be fooled? Her logic was impeccable, though her conclusions were incorrect.

Granted, this youngster was in a highly unusual situation. Yet, her plight was merely a more dramatic version of a phenomenon I have seen many times: students who couldn't tell who deserved the grades on their homework papers, school projects, or report cards, because their parents were so involved in teaching or doing the work.

Many youngsters in this situation react in another way. Rather than believing themselves to be inadequate, they display a clear-cut grandiosity. Despite deficient academic skills and motivation (and sometimes despite limited intellectual capacity), they have exaggerated notions about their academic prowess and plans for their future. They have high expectations for success, but no sense that they will have to exert effort to succeed. After all, experience has taught them that they can do well without doing anything at all.

When parents protect a student from failure, they also deprive him of the chance to learn how to deal with an important reality of life: Sometimes people fail even though they make a concerted, heart-felt effort. Doing work for a child who "has tried," so he won't "be punished" by a low or failing grade, does not help him learn that important truth. Failing is not a punishment. It is a disappointment. Repeatedly failing may mean we must either change our approach to our work, reset priorities, or establish new goals. By learning to deal with disappointments constructively, school children prepare for dealing with them later in life.

Protecting a student from failure teaches him that it doesn't really matter what he does or does not do. This can destroy a student's motivation. It destroys the motivation of other students, too, by making the measure of their success meaningless. Parents may not be too concerned about keeping their child's classmates motivated. However, they need to consider the effects their actions to prop up one child can have on the motivation of their other children.

Protecting a student from failure can diminish any good feelings that come when he does succeed. If the parent does much of the term paper for the child who would have passed the class in any case, the child cannot count his success as his own. A child with a conscience may continue to feel uncomfortable about having "cheated," or having received a grade he did not, in fact, deserve.

In the same way, protecting students from failure distorts their ideas about right and wrong. It is a small step from having a parent do one's work to having another student do one's work; from copying over a parent's essay in one's own handwriting to copying another student's essay in one's own handwriting. Is it possible to teach a child to steal and cheat when doing homework? Yes. Do parents do it? Unfortunately, some do.

Sometimes failing helps students develop a sense of what is truly important. It can help them realize that the deepest satisfaction is often derived from knowing they did the best job they could. Do your child a favor. Let him experience the consequences of his efforts.

Chapter 8

Special Considerations for Special Children

The Learning Disabled Child

Intervening to help an LD child with homework poses special difficulties. When setting up a homework program, parents face a number of contradictions. LD students usually find academic work very taxing. Expecting them to spend time studying after a hard school day may seem unreasonable or even unhealthy for a child. These students may also find homework harder, and it may take them longer to complete. Yet, unless they do the assignments, they risk falling even further behind. Many LD students dislike academics, because they must struggle so hard to complete assignments. Insisting they persist may lead them to dislike school-related tasks even more. On the other hand, people generally like things they do well. If a child is pressed to spend time studying, he may improve and grow to like school and learning.

It is common for LD students to receive very little homework in special education classes, and this can pose problems, too. Those who attend special education all day may never receive homework assignments. Reduced requirements make it harder to catch up, thus perpetuating a student's need for special help.

Despite these problems, learning disabilities are very popular these days, judging from the large numbers of students sporting the LD label and the many parents, teachers, and counselors striving to affix this particular diagnosis to their young charges. Students who are able to meet the LD criteria qualify by government mandate to receive special help. Usually this comes in the form of small classes with highly trained teachers. Special tutoring or summer programs may be available. It is therefore understandable that a diagnosis of learning disabled is such a widely sought commodity.

In fact, the search for a learning disability frequently begins as soon as a student has school problems, for if one can be found, special educational services become available. Often the hunt becomes a case of "seek and ye shall find." I have read countless evaluations where diagnosticians failed to uncover indications of a learning disability, but since the child was having academic problems, they diagnosed one anyway to obtain special services for the student!

I was very alarmed the first time a student who had been diagnosed learning disabled explained his diagnosis to me. "I've got something wrong with my brain," he told me. "I get things mixed up in my head. It means I can't learn even though I'm smart." I became even more alarmed as increasing numbers of students filed through my office year after year providing similar descriptions of their learning problems.

Understanding the way in which learning disabilities are assessed and diagnosed sheds light on the difficulties parents and students face when tackling homework problems.

■ **"I've got something wrong with my brain."** According to the *Diagnostic and Statistical Manual of Mental Disorders*, to diagnose an "academic skills disorder" (the technical name for learning disability),a student must not have a physical or neurological impairment that could explain the academic problems. However, most professionals believe LD children do have a neurological problem or minimal brain dysfunction, even though their medical tests are within normal range. Neurologists believe the tests are still too crude to identify the subtle problems that cause children to have difficulty learning. Most professionals remain convinced that organic abnormalities are responsible for many academic deficits. The catch-22 of this situation is that if a child does have neurological problems, he cannot technically be diagnosed learning disabled. If he has no neurological problems, he can be diagnosed learning disabled, yet everyone assumes he does have neurological problems!

■ **"I get things mixed up in my head."** Teachers suggest LD students "get things mixed up in their heads" in that they confuse left and right, read letters backwards or upside down, reverse letters when writing, have sloppy handwriting, have a hard time following more than one or two verbal instructions, or do poorly in one or two academic areas. The last category is a large one: It means that any student who is having trouble in a few subjects, but not all of them, may be considered learning disabled!

The problem with these criteria is that all young children reverse letters and words, have poor motor control, and have a hard time following several instructions. Some youngsters outgrow these behaviors more quickly than others. Students whose central nervous systems are less well-developed, either because they were born prematurely or because their biological clock ticks more slowly, progress less rapidly than children who mature at the usual rate. Children need lots of practice before they can grasp the fine distinctions between letters, develop the left-right habit, wield a pencil with grace, and learn basic mathematical and verbal concepts.

It has been hypothesized that if a youngster is understimulated during preschool years, he may miss a critical period for learning and can never overcome the early deprivation. This has not been proven. Many youngsters with little exposure to educational activities during preschool achieve normally or excel.

■ **"He can't learn even though he's smart."** According to federal guidelines, a learning disability may be diagnosed if a student's potential is higher than his achievement test scores. It is the difference between measures of intelligence and achievement that are relevant in making an LD diagnosis. If an IQ test shows a child to be a genius but the results of his achievement tests are merely above average, he may qualify for LD services, even though what he may need is a program for gifted children.

Of course, there are many reasons students can't learn even though they're smart. Just like adults, children who are depressed, anxious, or upset can't think clearly. Children from deprived backgrounds or troubled families often have a hard time putting much energy into school. Youngsters who are disorganized, impulsive, who don't behave in the classroom, can't work independently, or are uninterested in books, papers, and pencils don't do as well. Yet it is common for such children to be diagnosed as learning disabled.

The criteria for diagnosing learning disabilities differ from state to state and even from district to district. Many districts have diagnosed learning disabilities based on large differences between a student's verbal (language) and non-verbal (perceptual, visual-motor) abilities. Verbal skills are those which enable students to speak and understand oral and written material. Perceptual skills enable them to distinguish subtle differences in visual stimuli, such as the difference between a "b" and a "d"; visual-motor skills enable them to correctly see and reproduce such symbols.

If a student's test scores show him to be a genius at verbal tasks but only above average at visual-motor tasks (or vice versa), he may be diagnosed learning disabled. If he is above average in one area but only average in the other, he also meets the criteria. If he is equally poor in both verbal and non-verbal areas, he cannot qualify for special education services no matter how much he needs or wants help. The assumption is that normal children perform equally well in both verbal and non-verbal areas and that students who are much better in one area than the other are handicapped.

Why Johnny Can't Learn

The truth is that even professionals do not know why so many students have difficulties mastering basic skills. Nevertheless, thousands of students continue to be diagnosed to be suffering from a handicap for which there is supposedly little hope of recovery: The goal of special education programs is to teach students to compensate rather than overcome their deficiencies. The view that these students are handicapped persists even though many do become capable students.

Classroom teachers who have been in the business of teaching for a while have their own theories as to why increasing numbers of children have problems learning. They cite factors like large amounts of television viewing; increased numbers of children from chaotic, troubled, and deprived backgrounds; the prevalence of families in which both parents or the only parent works; inadequate preparation during preschool years; lack of training in the behaviors needed to control themselves in a classroom.

I believe it is significant that adults make the very same errors as do most learning disabled children when distracted or rushed. We transpose telephone numbers when taking messages, or dial "two" when we meant to dial "one." Even the most literate adult misreads signs, makes typing errors, writes a "q" when he means to write a "g," misinterprets the content of articles, gets confused when following oral or written directions. Those who take it slow and don't get distracted make fewer errors than those who are always running a race with an invisible clock or thinking about five things at once.

The fact is that students diagnosed learning disabled can and do learn. When provided with special services in small classrooms taught by highly trained teachers who emphasize experiential activities, most children not only improve but progress beyond the need for special education. Is the progress many students make due to the educational remediation targeted toward their specific handicap? Or is it because they get much needed attention, thrive in individualized programs with hands-on learning (which would seem the best method for teaching most students), and have a few extra years to develop physically and mature emotionally? Should the poor progress of other students be attributed to the fact that their handicap is so severe? Or is it because of the other problems that assert themselves once a child has been diagnosed learning disabled?

Helping An LD Child

Once a child has been diagnosed learning disabled, the label often takes on a life of its own. It becomes exceedingly difficult for parents and educators to maintain expectations, make reasoned decisions about homework, and implement study policies for a student who has been designated to be handicapped, whether or not he truly is. Parents' sympathetic feelings may lead them to reduce requirements, excuse youngsters from doing portions of the work, or do some of the work for them. Some parents become increasingly controlling. In their determination to cure the child by drilling, they insist he dedicate exorbitant amounts of time to doing school work at home. One father attempted to cure his son's poor handwriting by having him copy paragraphs from the encyclopedia for an hour each day.

Too often, the need to focus on weaknesses, problems, and deficits to assess and diagnose a learning disability (to justify inclusion in services for the handicapped) induces those working with the child to overlook his many strengths.

Even teachers who try to refrain from relating to an LD student as handicapped may react to the diagnosis. Parents cannot help but worry once the word "handicapped" has been used and references have been made to neurological impairment or brain damage. Many youngsters consider themselves incapable of mastering subjects after being told of their problems. Although parents and teachers may make efforts to reassure them of their abilities, the youngsters may absorb negative self-images from classmates. Peers see LD students as inadequate or unintelligent. This is true even though friends or family members can discern no difference. "I just found out my friend has a learning disability, and I was really shocked. I thought she was smart," a student told me.

Most parents find school conferences hard to face because discussions typically center around their child's handicap, deficits, and problems. While some parents increase their involvement at school, others stay away. Parent-teacher communication deteriorates, and the student's education may deteriorate. I have attended many school conferences, so I understand why parents may find them upsetting. I once accompanied parents to provide moral support. They had found previous meetings so painful they had not been able to bring themselves to meet with school personnel in quite some time. At the meeting, the school personnel gave a lengthy presentation detailing the youngster's problems. The parents looked increasingly upset. When they were finished, I asked if we could discuss the student's strengths. Indeed, there was a place on the special education forms for listing assets. There was an awkward pause, so I provided some examples of strengths I had observed. To the parents relief, the teachers and principal joined in. Soon the parents joined in, too. We were able to develop ideas for utilizing the student's strengths to formulate a much better school program for him.

Students who come to believe, "There's something wrong with my brain," "I can't learn even though I'm smart," "I get things mixed up in my head," or all three, are unlikely to believe their efforts to do homework assignments can really make a difference. The resulting attitudes make it harder to maintain motivation. It is imperative that parents of children with an LD diagnosis maintain the position that if the student continues to apply himself, he can and will progress.

How to Help an LD Child

■ **Never accept the idea that your child "can't learn."** Admit that the work is hard for him. Agree that it is frustrating. Allow him to be angry and cry about it. But don't excuse him from doing it!

■ **Encourage special education teachers to assign homework.** If students in mainstream classes receive homework, it is important that your child receive it, too. It's fine for assignments to be less demanding. But unless he receives regular assignments, he'll have fewer opportunities to master the many skills homework teaches so readily, such as remembering, budgeting time, working independently, and coping with responsibility. Students who don't receive homework assignments are at risk for falling further behind their peers.

■ **Help your child budget his study time so that he spends time every school night on difficult subjects.** The time need not be long. In setting up study periods and introducing the program, announce that a portion of his study period is to be spent on his difficult subjects. Say, "You will be having a study period that lasts twenty minutes each night. You will spend at least five minutes working on arithmetic, and the rest on your other school subjects."

If he is not receiving regular assignments, design activities which are appealing, interesting, rewarding, and fun. Find out what he is doing in his LD classes, and see if you can do similar activities at home. Many LD teachers rely on puzzles, games, and other fun materials to help students. Remember that students who like education will continue to pursue it for a lifetime.

■ **Continue educational activities during summer vacation.** Many districts offer summer enrichment programs for LD students which can provide the boost a student needs to make great strides. Remember that learning is a privilege, not a punishment, and help him value such special opportunities.

If no summer program is available, set aside fifteen to thirty minutes a day (depending on the age of the child) for developing skills in needed areas. Solicit recommendations from his teacher. Inexpensive workbooks, available at grocery stores or in the toy sections of department stores, provide excellent practice in basic skills and are designed so that most youngsters find them fun to do. Choose one which is not too challenging. Workbooks which are quite easy still provide opportunities to practice and strengthen basic skills, while building self-confidence and a sense of mastery.

■ **Find ways to integrate enjoyable opportunities to practice basic skills into your home.** If your child is having problems reading, point to each word as you read him his bedtime story. If he is having problems with comprehension, talk to him about the story as you read it. If he is having problems with verbal expression, listen more when he talks to you to encourage him to talk more and avoid correcting him. Instead, ask questions if you don't understand something. If he is having problems with math, use flash cards to make up games. Avoid drilling unless your child enjoys it.

■ **Develop a reward system, such as a "star chart," to provide extra incentive to work on academic areas your child finds difficult.** Post a paper on the refrigerator door and add a star or sticker every time he makes a good grade, does a neat paper, or does something extra in that subject. Make an agreement that when he gets ten stars, the family will do something special to celebrate. Remember that your child must like the rewards if they are to be motivating; if you make it too difficult for him to earn a star, he may end up feeling even more defeated.

■ **Discuss your youngster's difficulties in a frank, open, straightforward manner.** If you think you were remiss in providing the foundation necessary to do well in school during his preschool years, or if you think day-care personnel, nursery and preschool teachers, or baby-sitters provided inadequate preparation, talk about this. Say, "No one ever taught you the things you needed to know to prepare you for school. The school is going to give you extra help in a special class so you can catch up." Your child will benefit from having an explanation he can comfortably relate to peers.

If you believe emotional difficulties may account for the academic problems, share your impressions. Say, "Our family problems seem to have affected your school work. Extra help in a smaller class with a special teacher may help take some of the pressure off you for an hour or two during the school day."

If you do not know what has caused the problems, share that too. If your youngster has adopted the philosophy of "I can't learn because something's wrong with me," correct his misperception. Say, "In fact, no one knows why some students find it harder to learn than others, or find some subjects more difficult. If you spend more time practicing the things you find hard, you will improve."

If you believe the problems stem from slow physical maturation (as is often the case for premature babies) tell it like it is. Say, "Look, son. You walked late. You talked late. You're growing up a bit more slowly than a lot of other kids. You will probably catch up in a few years. In the meantime, your handwriting is going to be a bit sloppy and you may misread some words."

Have similar conversations with teachers to offset any despair about your child's ability. If your child was a premature infant, take time to talk about this. Discuss the effects on handwriting: Many teachers continue to press students about their handwriting even though the student simply lacks the motor control to write neatly. This discourages many students from doing homework. And don't hesitate to reassure your child that some things like handwriting will become less important for school success as he gets older.

■ **Control television watching!** Permit only educational programs to be viewed, or throw the T.V. out altogether! Every teacher I have talked to believes T.V. is the biggest educational liability for today's youth. "It teaches them to be passive," they say. "Instead of thinking, they sit and stare," they lament. "When I ask students to write or tell a story, all they do is repeat lines they've heard on T.V. They have no idea how to use their own minds or imaginations," they sigh.

■ **Schedule a school conference to determine whether your child is having problems with basic study skills.** Problems with organization, concentration, distractibility, perseverance, tolerance for frustration, and the abilities to plan ahead, structure time, and work independently are common underlying causes of learning problems. Look for problems with impulsivity and encourage your child to slow down and relax when tackling school work. Discuss your child's special strengths and areas of interest to help school personnel maintain a balanced view of your child.

■ **Consider the possibility that emotional problems are causing the school and homework problems.** Seek counseling if the school recommends it. Have your child evaluated by a psychologist if you are not sure. Many learning, concentration, and behavior problems are caused by depression and anxiety.

■ **Focus on small accomplishments and praise them to improve self-confidence.** Poor self-esteem is a major problem for students who are having academic problems, since so much of their life revolves around school.

The Hyperactive Child

"Attention deficit with hyperactivity disorder" is the latest term for children who have boundless energy. Like LD labels, ADHD labels are very popular these days because of the readily available public school services. Like LD diagnoses, solid medical information is lacking, but the general consensus among teachers, doctors, and counselors is that hyperactivity is an organic problem. Neurologists cite vague problems with "electrical wiring," while pediatricians and psychiatrists note unspecified "chemical imbalances." The consensus is that such children can't sit still, settle down, or concentrate. Medication is often recommended as a solution.

I remain unconvinced of the accuracy of this assumption. I am deeply concerned about the many students who are medicated and placed in special classes at school.

Personally, I meet all the criteria for "attention deficit disorder with hyperactivity" and so I consider myself a hyperactive adult. In truth, people must show symptoms before age 7 to be diagnosed hyperactive, and I was only active, not "hyper," as a child. My self-diagnosis is based on the actual criteria from the *Diagnostic and Statistical Manual of Mental Disorders,* third edition, revised, published by the American Psychiatric Association. All of the quoted material in the paragraph below appears on pages 52 and 53 of the manual:

When excited, I "often speak out of turn and interrupt." Some people say I "talk excessively." When I'm supposed to be writing this book I often "have difficulty sustaining attention" and end up thinking about other things. When I have to sit still at church, I often "fidget or squirm in my seat." I "don't follow instructions others give me" because "I don't listen well to what is being said to me" when somebody's telling me what to do. I "have a hard time completing chores" I don't like, "tending to jump from one uncompleted activity to another," and so I have a drawer full of unfinished articles and a closet of incomplete crafts projects. More often than I would like to admit, I "lose things necessary for tasks," especially pens, pencils, and car keys. I "often engage in physically dangerous activities for the purpose of thrill-seeking," like playing polo and show jumping my horse.

Yet I am content with the way I am. I enjoy working hard and playing hard. My affection for my "mental disorder" is another commonality I share with hyperactive children. As the *Diagnostic Manual* says, "This subclass of disorders is characterized by behavior that is socially disruptive and is often more distressing to others than to the people with the disorders." (page 49)

In fact, almost every ADHD-labeled child I have met was a lot like me. They may not be able to sit still at school, but they manage to concentrate on tasks they like. They may not get distracted from their favorite T.V. show, but they forget what they're supposed to be doing when told to do their homework. Their energy levels are high, unless they're exhausted or ill. They are happy with themselves except when others are telling them they should be different. They are irritating in the classroom unless their need to remain mentally or physically active is indulged.

Before you medicate your ADHD-child to settle him down, consider the results of the animal research I accidentally conducted and see whether my findings apply to your youngster's situation.

★ My horse needs lots of exercise. After cold weather made it necessary for him to stay in the barn for a few days, he began leaping and dashing in circles in his stall. He injured a leg as he bucked, but even that didn't slow him down. He simply had to relieve his pent up energy and could not wait — just as young children cannot sit still in school if they don't get enough time to play outside.

★ My cat slurped up some of my coffee before I could stop her. She spent the rest of the afternoon leaping on and off the counters, climbing the curtains, and attacking the dog. It was clear she was reacting to the caffeine in the coffee — just as children react to caffeine in colas and chocolate.

★ My dog becomes nervous if I'm upset, and races through the house barking at every tiny noise until I calm down. It is clear that she is reacting to my tension — just as children react to tension at home. If your home is mostly tense, your child may be mostly hyperactive. When you calm down, so may he.

★ I fed my bird a special high carbohydrate diet when she began molting. She became so wild after every feeding she shrieked and beat her wings against her cage until she broke many feathers and injured a wing. Clearly she was reacting to the carbohydrates — just as children react to sugar and starch.

To help an ADHD-student with homework:

■ Have him exercise long and hard before each study period. Provide a break half way through the study session and suggest he spend it riding his bicycle or running around the block.

■ Give him a snack before studying, if appropriate, but avoid foods containing sugar or caffeine for at least two hours prior to the study period.

■ Let him fidget and squirm in his chair. If you feel annoyed, look the other way. Nagging makes children more nervous, and increases the behavior you want to eliminate.

■ Continue to reset timers to compensate for interruptions during study periods, but don't nag!

■ Suggest he find short cuts and invent ways to do homework faster! This can be a productive way of channeling excess energy.

■ Give up hope of slowing him down. Instead, encourage him to put his ability to move fast and think quickly to good use. Consider shortening his study periods if he can do the work faster without sacrificing quality.

■ Discuss the importance of checking school work. It's the best way to compensate for the tendency to do things in a rush.

■ Accept the fact that he may need less sleep than others his age.

■ Spend extra time teaching study skills. Focus on teaching organizational skills and planning ability, as most hyperactive children have problems in these areas.

■ Remember that short-term remedies such as medication may lead to bigger problems in the long run. Medication may be helpful when combined with other interventions that help develop better internal controls, expend energy productively, and cope with anxieties. However, medication is unlikely to provide a permanent solution by itself.

■ Keep a diary to find patterns and causes for overactive behavior.

■ Encourage teachers to modify classroom policies to meet your energetic child's special needs. Students must sit still at times, but creative teachers can provide opportunities for movement. Classmates are not concerned (and are often relieved) when teachers make special rules for a particular student — it's easy for them to see that Johnny bothers everyone if he's forced to sit still. If the teacher designates your child "chief pencil sharpener," he may be able to get out of his seat ten to fifteen times a day. Perhaps your child can stand at a table instead of sitting at a desk. Even shifting his weight and moving around the table is a big help.

Most of all, try to view your child's exceptionally high energy level as a wonderful asset, and teach him how to take advantage of it. Certainly, that is what I do with mine!

The Emotionally Disturbed Child

Students who present serious emotional disturbances at school may be diagnosed emotionally disturbed and placed in special classes for children with behavioral problems. Those who remain quiet and refrain from bothering others are unlikely to be referred for special services, unless their classroom teacher is psychologically aware.

School psychologists are often reluctant to diagnose emotional disturbance, even if the child spends the school day conversing with spacemen or racing to the restroom to scrub imaginary germs from his hands. To do so may obligate school districts to provide self-contained classrooms at school, homebound teachers, or even educational programs in psychiatric hospitals to comply with the federal law requiring districts to provide a "free and appropriate public education." Providing these services is expensive. It is a credit to our country's commitment to universal education that schools continue to struggle to educate all children, although not all schools strive equally hard toward this ideal. Be sure your child is getting the services he is legally entitled to.

Parents of emotionally disturbed children share similar problems in getting their youngsters to do homework. They often feel uncertain about setting limits. When a child has many pressing problems, it is hard for parents to determine how hard to push to enforce rules. Making these decisions is not easy; there are no textbook answers. The child's personality and particular circumstances must be considered. Parents must try different approaches, assess the student's reaction, and decide when to abandon a technique as counterproductive, and when to give the youngster more time to adjust.

It is very difficult for parents to remain sufficiently objective to determine when to forge ahead and when to back off. Some youngsters become hysterical when a parent tries to set limits and enforce homework rules. Is this a manipulation? Or is the youngster truly overwhelmed? In both cases, the child may seem quite content as soon as the parent backs off. Is this because the child won a battle? Is it because the child is relieved that the parent understands how truly overwhelmed he was and feels better now that some pressure has been removed? To make the wrong decision can make a bad situation worse. But how to make a good one?

Parents need advice and support from someone they trust. Sometimes teachers or school counselors are good resources. Many mental health agencies provide special parenting classes. Support groups enable parents to exchange ideas and receive ongoing feedback and emotional support.

What should a parent to do to help an emotionally disturbed child with homework? There are no easy answers, and parents need to decide what fits their individual situation. Nevertheless, I recommend that parents implement a homework program. I have known many children who responded well to having this routine and structure in their otherwise chaotic lives. Many of the techniques employed in this study program are used in hospital psychiatric programs to help adolescent patients improve study skills and do homework.

The Withdrawn Child

Draw a child who is lost in the world of his own fantasies back to reality by touching him gently and saying, "Johnny, it may be hard to study and do homework right now, but it is important that you try." Praise him each and every time he writes a sentence or completes a problem, regardless of the quality of the work. The first goal is to help him attend to the task at hand and build his confidence. Only after he is working steadily should you withhold praise for quantity and provide approval and hugs for quality.

The Aggressive Child

If your child becomes angry and verbally abusive when you announce the beginning of a study period, simply turn the other cheek. Don't defend yourself, cry, or beg forgiveness for being such a mean parent. Don't become a mean parent by acting angry or abusive. Guard your tendency to react to words like never (as in "I'll never study, and you can't make me!") and forever (as in "I'll hate you forever for doing this to me!").

Remain firm and unbending by simply timing the tantrum and lengthening the study period. Stay up all night if you have to, and enforce the rule about sleeping during a study period. After about five consecutive days of tantrumless pouting (usually without any studying, though), congratulate your child on his self-control. Encourage him to take the next step by saying, "I always knew you had it in you to control your anger. I'm sure you can let go of your anger, so you can use your time to study, too." This may well result in a new round of tantrums. As soon as these tantrums end, many students immediately begin to work.

The Depressed Child

If your child becomes upset and threatens to hurt himself when you announce the beginning of a study period, remain compassionate but firm. Say, "I'm concerned that you feel so upset about studying that you would actually think about injuring or killing yourself. I would feel terrible if anything happened to you. We will have your study period, and I will stay up all night to watch you to make sure you are safe. Tomorrow we will find a professional who can help with these problems." Then don't let your child out of your sight even if you are convinced he is just "crying wolf," until you find someone who can see him for an emergency evaluation. Call the school in the morning, and discuss the problem with a counselor to obtain recommendations for getting help.

Threats of self-injury are usually manipulations, but the high rate of suicide among teenagers makes every threat serious. Even if suicidal threats are merely attempts to manipulate, the best strategy may still be to conduct the study period while treating the threats with the utmost seriousness. If your child really had no intentions of harming himself, he'll think twice before using such a manipulation again. If he did, you'll ensure that he is protected.

Sociopathic Children

Youngsters who lack a conscience and have no discernable desire to please parents or conform to the dictates of authority may be especially resistant to doing homework. They usually remain unmoved by parental expressions of concern, may be notably indifferent to praise, and are more likely than others to behave aggressively or in passive-aggressive ways when criticized or punished. Such youngsters are apt to comply and conform only when they want to do so. When it comes to homework they may never voluntarily comply.

Even though they may make progress to the point of spending their study sessions doing homework, it is hard to motivate them to work independently. The moment the structure is decreased and the parent's back is turned, they do something else instead of studying.

Parents must often resign themselves to providing continuous personal monitoring of study periods. The alternative may be to institute a continuing system of rewards. The rewards must be immediate: at the end of each study period, never more than a week away. They must be truly attractive to the child, which means the parent may need to change them often. A reward allowing the youngster to watch T.V. for an hour won't help if there is nothing on television he wants to see.

Rewards must be planned and shared with the child in advance. If you suddenly up your demands and inform him that now instead of receiving a reward for simply studying, he must also achieve certain grades, he may become angry and resist the urge to achieve rewards he would like to have. Share your preliminary plans with his teachers, solicit their input, and try to have all possible problems ironed out before presenting the plan to your child. Develop a program that looks something like this:

Week 1:   Reward on days he brings his book home and arrives to study sessions on time.
Week 2:   Reward on days he studies.
Week 3:   Reward on days he completes assignments, turns them in, and receives all passing grades. (You will have to obtain feedback from teachers to know that he did pass. Do not count on receiving accurate reports from the child.)
Week 4:   Reward on days he receives all passing grades on assignments and tests.
Week 5:   Reward on days he receives grades his teachers consider reasonable for him to make (no grade lower than a C, for instance).

Sociopathic children can be very difficult to deal with, and even most professionals admit to having few answers as to how to help. The challenge appears to be establishing an emotional connection and winning their trust. The general consensus is that providing a tight structure to create boundaries on their behavior works best.

Despite the widely accepted view that such youngsters are unresponsive to parental expressions of caring and concern, many do show sporadic signs of wanting to please, and it is important to remain alert to these all-important signs. Encourage your child by taking pleasure in and remarking on things he does that are pleasing to you or others.

Most of all, try to get your child to see that people really care and can give to one another, but hold him to the limits you establish. Let him know you care and that you wish you could give him the rewards—even if he didn't earn them — but that you cannot. At the core of these children's problems is a marked inability to comprehend that people care even though they don't always satisfy personal desires.

Shadow Children

Bringing up the rear of the academic ability spectrum are shadow children. This is a euphemism for "children who are not very bright." They look like normal children. They act like normal children. However, they have limited ability to learn academics. Their IQ test scores range from about 70 to 80, so they are far below average, functioning in the dull-normal range. Their intelligence level isn't low enough to qualify them to receive special education services for the mentally retarded (developmentally delayed) or high enough to qualify them for help given to students who are having trouble in just one or two academic areas (learning disabled). They fall between the cracks of the educational system and are confined to regular (mainstream) classrooms without special assistance, despite their inability to keep up. Shadow children are often misdiagnosed, especially if they have good social skills.

One set of parents sought therapy for their daughter at the insistence of her high school counselor who was concerned about her failing grades. "She's just not trying." "She's capable of more." "She just won't do the work." "She's insufficiently motivated." Thus read the notes in her permanent folder which spanned many years. Her parents were at their wit's end. "Please find out what's wrong with her!" they begged. So I asked the daughter what was wrong with her. "Like they say — I'm lazy," she smiled. A few minutes later it became apparent that all this teenager ever had to say was exactly what someone else had just said. She had learned to smile and nod and repeat the endings of other people's sentences to hold up her end of the conversation. She knew how to dress, how to behave, how to watch others and do what they did. She did not know how to think for herself, how to read a fifth grade textbook (actually she could read quite well; she just didn't know what any of the words meant), or how to calculate the number of days between Friday and Tuesday. Despite keen powers of observation and excellent social skills, her performance during an extensive evaluation supported my hypothesis: She was darling, but she was intellectually deficient.

Shadow children can learn to read, write, and do arithmetic, along with almost everything else in elementary school. It takes them a lot longer, they must struggle twice as hard, but they can and do learn the basics. Their grades often plunge from below average to failing in middle school unless they are placed in remedial classes. They often thrive in high school vocational and work-study programs, and can certainly go on to live normal lives, holding jobs, getting married and raising children. In the meantime, school is an extraordinarily difficult, frustrating experience for them from kindergarten on unless the academic standards at their school are exceptionally low.

How do you help your shadow child with homework? Here are some suggestions.

★ Be lavish in praising efforts. It is most important that he keep trying. Help him fight the urge to give up that often results from receiving consistently poor grades.

★ Confront teachers who suggest your child is capable of more and ask for proof. Just as it is harmful to expect too little from a student, it is harmful to expect too much.

★ Resign yourself to seeking a tutor who can work with him on a permanent basis or work with your child yourself, if you can remain kind and patient as you do so. You will do damage, if you become frustrated when he is slow to catch on. If you can't remain tolerant, find a tutor.

★ If he is getting along well with his peers, consider carefully before holding him back in school. He may have difficulties adjusting to a new set of classmates, and his grades will probably not improve. On the other hand, he may relate better to younger children, and may learn more the second time.

★ Do not shorten study periods. Even though school may be a grueling, frustrating experience for your shadow child, it is imperative that he master the basics and learn as much as he can.

★ Be realistic in your expectations, but don't baby him. Expect C's in elementary school, with only an occasional D, unless the academic level of his school is much higher or lower than the national average.

★ Expend extra efforts to teach the study skills discussed in chapter 7. Concentration, planning ability, perseverance, and organization will be crucial to his future job success. These skills can go a long way toward compensating for deficits in other areas.

★ Be sure he knows how to confront others and stand up for his rights.

★ Watch for signs of emotional and/or adjustment difficulties, and attend to them sooner rather than later. It is not easy being different when the difference is you're less intelligent than almost everyone else. Peers are prone to scapegoat slower children, while adults often pity or misunderstand them. Unless your shadow child is especially charming or attractive, getting along socially may be as hard as getting along academically.

Gifted Children

Sometimes it is easy to spot academically gifted students. They make mostly A's. They do all the extra credit work. They are voracious readers. Adults are readily impressed by their wealth of knowledge, precocious observations, and in-depth grasp of a particular subject or subjects. Such children usually top the charts on standardized achievement and IQ tests.

Sometimes it is hard to spot an academically gifted child. Their grades range from slightly above average to failing. They do as little as possible at school. They hate to read. They keep their thoughts to themselves, so adults see them as ordinary, everyday kids. Even though they top the charts on achievement and IQ tests, no one thinks much about their scores — unless their daily grades are exceptionally poor. In that case, teachers may note, "he could do better if he tried," "he's an underachiever," or "he's not working up to his potential." The child is usually branded as unmotivated or lazy.

I have seen so many children whose homework and school problems stem from the fact that they are "too bright" that I believe this problem deserves national attention. It is ironic that even as we bemoan the academic deficiencies of American youth, we fail to provide educational opportunities for those who are able and often willing to do more.

Many academic wizards are like sponges: They soak up every ounce of information doled out at school and then some. Some teachers enjoy having such students in their classes and willingly extend themselves to aid and abet the development of their special potential. Unfortunately, many teachers don't devote time to designing special learning experiences to keep exceptionally bright students challenged. Further, it is common for teachers to feel threatened and react with hostility to precocious children. Gifted students may catch teacher errors, ask questions teachers cannot answer, or know more about some subjects than the teacher. Classmates quickly absorb negative teacher attitudes and it is common for exceptionally bright students to be scapegoated and ostracized at school.

The number one school problem of academically gifted children is boredom. Imagine what it is like for a child reading on the sixth grade level to sit through a reading group on the first grade level, being forced to listen to classmates stumble over the same words he mastered long ago. Imagine him having to write out all the steps to every mathematics problem when he knows the answer just by looking at them. And imagine, too, that he is reprimanded for not paying attention when his eyes fall closed, when he looks out the window, when he doodles to try to stay awake, and when he is caught reading books or engaging in an academic activity different from everyone else.

Most classrooms have strict rules. It is not enough for a student to remain quiet and refrain from disturbing others: He must do what the rest of the class is doing, whether he needs to be doing it or not! Even when school work is self-paced and children are allowed to work at their own speed, they must still complete all thirty math problems on page 157 of the textbook even though they only need to do ten to get enough practice. Very few programs are truly individualized.

Programs for talented and gifted children are few and far between. Those that do exist are often inadequate to meet students' needs. Many classroom teachers are reluctant to allow exceptionally bright students to work ahead, since it demands so much of the teacher's time. As one teacher said, "I wouldn't mind letting him work at his own pace, but he could probably finish the entire year's worth of work in a few months. What would I do with him then?"

Children who are allowed to skip grades may develop social problems, because intellectual prowess and emotional maturity are entirely different. An ability to solve calculus problems does not mean a child can grasp the subtle points of social interactions necessary to win friends and influence enemies.

Even when the school day is over the child can't leave it behind. Homework, which is about as boring as the school day is long, has been assigned. He must write every spelling word five times — it doesn't matter that he already knows how to spell them all. He is to complete countless worksheets to practice the new material he didn't learn that day (because he already knew it). Many gifted children are very obstinate about doing homework. It is hard to blame them.

Some gifted students tune out the goings-on in the classroom and tune into their own fantasies to relieve boredom. They may tune out so much of the time that they miss vital material. Their grades decline. Sometimes their achievement test scores decline as well, and they actually fall behind other children. They may come into their own years later, when the work is more challenging, or they may develop such an intense dislike for school, they drop out at an early age.

What should you do if you end up having to cope with the educational problems of an exceptionally bright student? The first step is to discuss the problem with your child. Otherwise, he may be hurt by comments from threatened teachers and jealous classmates and lose confidence. He may come to see himself as others see him and decide he is "lazy," "unmotivated," or "a trouble maker," rather than "too bored" because he is "too smart."

Next, it is important to do what you can to encourage your school district and his classroom teachers in particular to accommodate his special needs. Usually accelerated and honors classes are available for middle and high school students. The challenge is to keep your child motivated to continue learning until the school environment has more to offer. Otherwise, he may not even qualify for the extra opportunities once they become available.

Schedule a school conference to discuss your child's special educational needs. Many parents refrain from taking action because they are afraid school personnel will think they are bragging. Ask yourself which is worse: to be seen as a doting parent or to let your child down by not confronting the problem? I suggest parents say something like, "I'm concerned that my child is not being exposed to material that will encourage him to fulfill his potential. I'd like to discuss ways that his special needs may be accommodated."

Check to see if your school has a policy that states that the individual needs of each student are to be provided for. If one exists and you cannot obtain cooperation from your school, contact the superintendent. Explore every outside learning opportunity you can find by talking to the district office. There may be experimental programs, magnet schools, or enrichment programs which the classroom teacher or even school principal is not aware of.

Brainstorm possible solutions and see if the teacher is amenable to implementing them. Here are some possibilities:

★ Allow the student to go to the library, work on special projects in the classroom, or read books when classmates are learning material he already knows.

★ Provide opportunities for independent study, perhaps with community volunteers overseeing the study.

★ Provide self-paced learning materials whenever possible, and make sure they are challenging.

★ Have the student tutor slower classmates. Teaching others will encourage him to think about various ways of conceptualizing the problems and solidify his understanding of the material.

★ Allow the student to participate as a teacher's helper by grading tests and assignments, leading discussions, handing out and collecting papers. These activities can relieve boredom, develop leadership skills, and control behavior problems.

★ Cut back on homework assignments to meet the child's needs. If he needs less repetition to learn, have him do every other math problem rather than every one.

★ Exempt the student from doing homework which is too easy and instead, require similar but more demanding work. For instance, rather than requiring him to copy spelling words, have him write a story that uses them all. Rather than doing the assigned math problems, have him work out of a supplemental text.

Unfortunately, not only is public school programming often inadequate for these children, but if a gifted student has received poor grades because he fails to complete homework or spends time fantasizing or misbehaving during the day, it is often difficult to even convince teachers that he is very bright. Some parents move to a district whose system nurtures gifted as well as disabled learners. Some families use Aunt Edith's address to gain illegal entry into the school across town with the experimental program for whiz kids. Others beg for scholarships or borrow from relatives to get their child into a more demanding educational setting. So what do you, as the parent of such a child, do about homework? Do you insist he complete assignments which are clearly a waste of his time? Do you support teachers' demands that he harness his creativity and complete work in the manner prescribed?

I believe that is usually best. Just as students who have poor frustration tolerance must learn to persevere, so must academically gifted children. Throughout their lives they have to cope with the boredom that stems from having to wait for others to catch up or catch on. The need to cope with peers and superiors who are jealous of their capabilities and who react by trying to thwart or undermine their progress won't disappear over time.

Discuss these issues with your child in a straightforward, direct manner. You need not worry about him becoming conceited if you tell him the truth: "Your special talents are wonderful assets. They may open doors which are closed to others, and take you far in life. Your special talents are also great handicaps. They make your life more difficult. You must learn to cope with boredom, to have patience with those less bright, to deal with the jealousy of others."

Seek ways to nurture his special gift. Attend school board meetings and lobby for special programming. Join national organizations to support the cause of talented and gifted students (they often have information about special programs, too). If no local chapters exist in your area, start one! Investigate programs offered by community colleges — many provide programs for younger students. YMCA's, libraries, as well as colleges and universities offer adult education classes, but actually have no age requirements for those wishing to attend. Encourage independent learning at home and provide opportunities to explore personal interests rather than following yours. If his in-school program is inadequate, he may already spend more than enough time doing work he doesn't enjoy.

Most of all, treasure his special gift, that he may treasure it, too.

Compulsive Studiers

Our society reveres those who are especially dedicated and achievement-oriented, so it is common for parents, teachers, and peers to overlook the plight of a driven student. In fact, such students are usually admired for their dedication and determination to do better than their best. Those who are bright receive many honors for their outstanding scholastic accomplishments. Since the compulsion to study usually develops over time rather than all at once, it is easy to miss when a student has lost control of his drive to excel, and it has become a force that is driving him instead.

■ **Emotional problems.** Compulsive studiers are very different from students who simply enjoy studying and strive to do their best. They study to avoid other problems, so doing homework functions as a coping mechanism. Although they may claim to love school, these homework fanatics are generally tense, unhappy, and reticent about sharing their distress.

Since they equate their worth as human beings with scholastic success, a poor grade is a serious blow. It is common for them to become depressed when they do not meet their exacting standards. During adolescence they may become suicidal, so it is critical for those involved with such students to respond to their expressions of despair. This can be difficult to do, for it is usually hard for others to fathom that someone could actually be so distraught over a poor grade, especially when the grade is a B on a relatively insignificant paper.

To further complicate matters, some academic superstars extend their zeal to extracurricular activities. These students have a variety of interests and involvements, and may be popular with peers. This makes it almost impossible for others to empathize with the many self-doubts that plague them. It can be hard to comprehend their conviction that disaster has struck just because they are unprepared for a test, or understand that they could take a single defeat so seriously when they are clearly succeeding in so many areas.

Despite the popularity of many compulsive studiers, their relationships tend to be superficial. Their tendency to keep an emotional distance stems from their feelings of inadequacy. Even those who have many academic successes have problems with self-esteem. This is due to their conviction that they must achieve to be deserving of another's love. *For most of these students, the real need is to feel lovable whether or not they excel.*

A compulsive approach to studying works to a youngster's emotional detriment. Although burying oneself in homework may provide an escape from other problems, it does nothing to resolve them and often compounds them. Studying to compensate for perceived social inadequacies by excelling at academics means the youngster has less opportunity to develop social skills. Although studying may help a youngster feel better in the short-run, no amount of studying or academic success solves the core problem: the need to feel accepted for who one is, rather than what one accomplishes.

Compulsive studying, like other kinds of compulsive behavior, creates problems of its own, and may cause serious academic, physical, and family problems.

■ **Academic problems.** Like their adult workaholic counterparts, home-work fanatics pay a high price for their all-consuming preoccupation. Despite the incredibly long hours these students put into doing homework and studying, they actually accomplish less than if they adopted a more relaxed approach. Most work sporadically rather than consistently, study-ing endlessly for a few days, then collapsing and doing nothing. It may be so hard for them to face school with an incomplete assignment, they would rather be absent than risk exposure.

Working so hard causes them to feel tired much of the time and interferes with their ability to think clearly. They make many careless errors and spend exorbitant amounts of time focusing on irrelevant details of assignments. Many show symptoms of burnout at a young age: Overnight they may lose interest in school, and their grades can drop dramatically in a very short time. Although often reprimanded for not working up to capacity, in fact, the problem is they are working above it.

■ **Physical problems.** Because they are literally addicted to studying, they are unable to bring themselves to sleep, relax, play, and take care of themselves. The continued state of exhaustion causes them to miss a lot of school. Absences are necessitated by their very real need to compensate for lost sleep. They may also suffer psychosomatic illnesses such as asthma, headaches, allergies, or ulcers. Being generally run-down in-creases their susceptibility to viruses and infections.

Problems with insomnia are common, as are nightmares. Being exposed as a sham or missing an exam are common themes even in their dreams. They may get little rest even when they sleep for long hours.

■ **Family problems.** It is common for another family member to display emotional disturbance which preclude providing emotional support. The child's craving for affirmation is satisfied at school, and he develops a strong incentive to achieve. Compulsive study habits often begin when the child identifies with an adult who values education and encourages achieve-ment. The adult may be a parent, a teacher, a camp counselor, choir master, coach, girl scout leader, or a family friend. The successes are reinforcing, and temporarily forestall the emotional hunger these youngsters experience.

Parents of homework fanatics are usually seen as either pushing their child to succeed or as trying to undermine their child's success, if they express concerns. Some parents do place extreme pressure on their children to achieve, reinforcing the child's notion that his worth is tied to his ability to perform academically. The tendency to push youngsters into academics at increasingly early ages may increase the incidence of compulsive behaviors. It is hard to know for sure. Certainly, parents who dwell on achievement rather than a youngster's overall well-being are overlooking his deeper needs.

Although many youngsters become compulsive achievers in response to parental pressures, this is not necessarily the cause. In fact, many parents are at the opposite extreme: They remain oblivious to their child's achievements, while he continues to study zealously in hopes of finally winning parental recognition or approval.

In between are the many parents who want their child to do well in school but are troubled by their youngster's compulsion to study. They are acutely aware that their child is unhappy and try to find ways to help him pursue a more reasonable and balanced approach to school work. They may encourage him to relax more, study less, and try to help solve the underlying problems. Sorting out what causes youngsters to behave as they do is often impossible. Parents who solicit professional help are often disappointed in the results. Problems with compulsive studying are often quite intransigent to traditional forms of therapy. It may be that programs following the Alcoholic's Anonymous model which have helped so many control their addictions could prove a viable alternative.

Helping A Homework Fanatic

Parents of homework fanatics cannot solve their children's problems for them. Like parents of students with other types of problems, all they can do is establish conditions to promote a healthy approach to studying. The rest is up to the child.

Most of these children need help limiting the amount of time they spend on homework. This is especially true for students who overindulge in studying at certain times, then are too burned-out, ill, and exhausted to attend school.

Limiting the amount of time they spend doing homework has several benefits. Parents send a clear message that there is more to life than studying. They help safeguard their child's physical health. They encourage the child to prioritize work and focus on important assignments.

Setting these limits is not without problems, and for some students there is even an element of risk. A student who bases his worth on his grades may lose his sense of purpose, even his desire to go on living, if prevented from achieving at his expected levels. Before imposing time restrictions, follow the recommendations below. Even then, consider carefully, and watch for signs that the child is experiencing the intevention as a major source of stress.

★ Since homework fanatics may study to the point of endangering their health, parents must set and enforce reasonable bedtimes. It can be the parent's way of saying, "Your health matters more to me than your homework!"

★ Compulsive studiers rarely require monitored study periods. It is usually more beneficial for parents to put their energy into spending time with their child on activities that do not involve school work. Encourage your child to have fun. Talk to him about his tendency to negate his playful side by turning activities into win/ lose propositions.

★ Although most homework fanatics can study in their bedrooms, it may be helpful to insist they study in a central location with a parent nearby. Withdrawn youngsters may benefit from being pulled back into the family.

★ Note if your child knows how to prioritize work, budget time, plan ahead, and persevere. Provide help if needed.

★ Remind child often that you love him. If he is upset over a grade or less-than-perfect paper, talk about aspects of his personality that you and others find endearing and special.

★ Respond to his academic successes by sharing his delight, but take care to remind him that his ability to achieve scholastically is only one of the many things you value about him.

★ Talk to your child about things that are troubling him, and encourage him to confront and seek solutions to his problems. If he is reluctant to talk, spend more time together and seek to strengthen your relationship.

★ Encourage him to reach out to friends and accept friendship. A network of friends can go a long way toward satisfying his emotional hunger, and is especially important for adolescents.

★ Avoid responding critically when he makes a mistake.

★ Become involved in a self-help group if another family member suffers from addictive behaviors such as chemical dependency, eating or spending disorders, or other forms of addiction.

★ Seek immediate professional help if your child becomes overly despondent or makes suicidal statements, even if they are expressed as vague "wonderings" about what it would be like to be dead. The self-induced academic pressures and internal expectations for perfection can become truly overwhelming, and too many compulsive students seek drastic solutions to obtain relief.

Homework
Survey

Dear Teacher,

In order to help my child with school, I am starting a homework program as suggested in the book, *The Homework Solution*. To determine how long my youngster, _____, needs to study and do homework each evening, I need some information about your homework and study policies. I would appreciate your taking a moment to answer the questions below.

1. How often do you usually assign homework? _____.

2. Do you often assign homework on weekends and over school holidays?

3. Although homework assignments change from day to day, how long should my child plan to spend studying and doing homework on a daily basis?

4. Please list some things my child needs to pay attention to when doing homework and studying.

5. Does my child have problems in any of the areas listed below? Please circle those that are problems.

   a. Impulsivity
   b. Concentration
   c. Distractibility
   d. Planning ability (thinking ahead)
   e. Budgeting time (using time wisely)
   f. Organization
   g. Tolerance for frustration
   h. Perseverance
   i. Overly perfectionistic
   j. Working independently
   k. Handling responsibility
   l. Initiative
   m. Other _____

Please let me know if your policies on homework change. I may be reached at _____. Feel free to call to discuss this further.

Sincerely,

_____

Parent's
Progress
Journal

I.   Time study period started.

Name of student	Set timer	Grade	Comments

II.   Minutes late to study period.

Name of student	Minutes	Grade	Comments

III.   Complaints.

Name of student	#	Grade	Comments

IV.   Brought study materials.

Name of student	Yes/No	Grade	Comments

V.   Delays in studying.

Name of student	Set timer	Grade	Comments

VI.   Interruptions caused by the student.

Name of student	#	Grade	Comments

VII. Outside interruptions.

Name of student	#	Grade	Comments

VIII. End of study period.

Name of student	Minutes	Grade	Comments

IX.   Voluntary study.

Name of student	Minutes	Grade	Comments

X.   Helping breaks.

Name of student	Minutes	Grade	Comments

XI.   Parental self-evaluation.

Name of student	#	Grade	Comments

XIII. Plans.

Goal	Grade

Appendix C

Teacher
Feedback Form

Dear Teachers: I am seeking information regarding _____'s school work from _____ to _____, 199__. Please provide the information below to help me determine whether my child's homework and studying skills are improving, staying the same, or declining. Call me if you have questions or comments.

Sincerely,

Name of subject	Were homework assignments Complete or Incomplete (Circle "C" or "I")	Test, quiz & daily grades	Comments
_____	C —	— —	_____
_____	C —	— —	_____
_____	C —	— —	_____
_____	C —	— —	_____
_____	C —	— —	_____
_____	C —	— —	_____
_____	C —	— —	_____
_____	C —	— —	_____

Student Planner

Day/Date _____

Homework:

Subject	Assignment	Special instructions	Time	Order	Completed	Grade

Special projects & tests:

Subject	Assignment	Special instructions	Date due

Items to take home:

Books, materials, & supplies	Miscellaneous

More good books from
WILLIAMSON PUBLISHING

To order additional copies of *The Homework Solution,* please enclose $10.95 per copy plus $2.50 shipping and handling. Follow "To Order" instructions on the last page. Thank you.

PARENTS ARE TEACHERS, TOO
Enriching Your Child's First Six Years
by Claudia Jones

Be the best teacher your child ever has! Jones shares hundreds of ways to help any child learn in playful home situations. Lots on developing reading, writing, math skills. Plenty on creative and critical thinking, too. A book you'll love using!

192 pages, 6 x 9, illustrations, quality paperback, $9.95

<u>MORE</u> PARENTS ARE TEACHERS, TOO
Encouraging Your 6- to 12-Year-Old
by Claudia Jones

Help your children be the best they can be! When parents are involved, kids do better. When kids do better, they feel better, too. Here's a wonderfully creative book of ideas, activities, teaching methods and more to help you help your children over the rough spots and share in their growing joy in achieving. Plenty on reading, writing, math, problem-solving, creative thinking. Everything for parents who want to help but not push their children.

226 pages, 6 x 9, illustrations, quality paperback, $10.95

THE KIDS' NATURE BOOK
365 Indoor/Outdoor Activities and Experiences
by Susan Milord

Winner of the Parents' Choice Gold Award for learning and doing books, *The Kids' Nature Book* is loved by children, grandparents, and friends alike. Simple projects and activities emphasize fun while quietly reinforcing the wonder of the world.

160 pages, 12 x 9, 425 illustrations, quality paperback, $12.95

KIDS CREATE!
Art & Craft Experiences for 3- to 9-year-olds
by Laurie Carlson

What's the most important experience for children ages 3 to 9? Creating something by themselves ranks among the best. Carlson provides over 150 creative experiences ranging from making dinosaur sculptures to clay cactus gardens, from butterfly puppets to windsocks. Plenty of help for the parents working with the kids, too! A delightfully innovative book.

160 pages, 11 x 8½, over 400 illustrations, quality paperback, $12.95

ADVENTURES IN ART
Art & Craft Experiences for 7- to 14-year-olds
by Susan Milord

Imagine an art book that encourages children to explore, to experience, to touch and to see, to learn and to create . . . imagine a true adventure in art. Here's a book that teaches artisan's skills without stifling creativity. Covers making handmade papers, puppets, masks, paper seascapes, seed art, tin can lantern, berry ink, still life, silk screen, batiking, carving and so much more. Let the adventure begin!

160 pages, 11 x 8½, 500 illustrations, quality paperback, $12.95

THE BROWN BAG COOKBOOK:
Nutritious Portable Lunches for Kids and Grown-Ups
by Sara Sloan

Here are more than 1,000 brown bag lunch ideas with 150 recipes for simple, quick, nutritious lunches that kids will love. Breakfast ideas, too! This popular book is now in its sixth printing!

192 pages, 8¼ x 7¼, illustrations, quality paperback, $8.95

Easy-to-Make
TEDDY BEARS AND ALL THE TRIMMINGS
by Jodie Davis

Now you can make the most lovable, huggable, plain or fancy teddy bears imaginable, for a fraction of store-bought costs. Step-by-step instructions and easy patterns drawn to actual size for large, soft-bodied bears, quilted bears, and even jointed bears. Plus patterns for clothes, accessories – even teddy bear furniture!

192 pages, 8½ x 11, illustrations and patterns, quality paperback, $12.95

GOLDE'S HOMEMADE COOKIES
by Golde Soloway

Over 50,000 copies of this marvelous cookbook have been sold. Now its in its second edition with 135 of the most delicious cookie recipes imaginable. *Publisher Weekly* says, "Cookies are her chosen realm and how sweet a world it is to visit." You're sure to agree!

162 pages, 8¼ x 7¼, illustrations, quality paperback, $8.95

DOING CHILDREN'S MUSEUMS:
A Guide to 265 Hands-On Museums, Revised and Expanded
by Joanne Cleaver

Turn an ordinary day into a spontaneous "vacation" by taking a child to some of the 265 participatory children's museums, discovery rooms, and nature centers covered in this highly acclaimed, one-of-a-kind book. Filled with museum specifics to help you pick and plan the perfect place for the perfect day.

232 pages, 6 x 9, quality paperback, $13.95

To Order:

At your bookstore or order directly from Williamson Publishing. We accept Visa and MasterCard (please include number and expiration date) or check. Send to:

Williamson Publishing Company
Church Hill Road, P.O. Box 185
Charlotte, Vermont 05445

Toll-free phone orders with credit cards: 1-800-234-8791
Please add $2.50 per order for shipping. Satisfaction guaranteed!